The Fruit of Silence

*The Jesus Prayer as a Foundation
to the Art of Spiritual Life*

Third Edition

Edward Kleinguetl

**outskirts
—— press**

Outskirts Press, Inc.
http://www.outskirtspress.com

ISBN: 978-1-9772-2287-9

Cover photos: The Pantocrator and Russian Chapel in Antarctica are used under license from iStock. Other pictures are used with permission or are public domain.

Previously published as *Hearts Afire: A Personal Encounter with Jesus*
First edition   2013
Second edition   2015
Third edition   2020

Outskirts Press and the "OP" logo are trademarks belonging to Outskirts Press, Inc.

PRINTED IN THE UNITED STATES OF AMERICA

The fruit of silence is prayer.

—St. Teresa of Calcutta

The prayer of the mind is the highest school of theology.

—Nicephorus the Solitary

The first words of the Savior to fallen mankind were: "Repent, for the kingdom of heaven is at hand" (Matt. 4:17). Therefore, until you enter the kingdom, knock at its doors through repentance and prayer.

—St. Ignatius Brianchaninov

The chief preoccupation of all disciples of Jesus must be their sanctification. The first place in their lives must be given to prayer, to silent contemplation, and to the Eucharist …

—Robert Cardinal Sarah

We need to pray and we need to teach people to pray.

—Bishop Milan Lach, SJ

IMPRIMATUR

+ Daniel Cardinal DiNardo, DD
Archbishop of Galveston-Houston
June 4, 2002

For His Excellency Most Rev. Joseph E. Strickland, Bishop of Tyler,
who has consistently and courageously stood in opposition
to those who propose to dilute the Deposit of Faith and
who seek compromise with the spirit of the age.
Further, through personal witness, he regularly demonstrates
the importance of prayer in the renewal of the Church.

O God, who willed that our infirmities
be borne by your Only Begotten Son
to show the value of human suffering,
listen in kindness to our prayers
for our brothers and sisters who are sick;
grant that all who are oppressed by
pain, distress or other afflictions
may know that they are chosen
among those proclaimed blessed
and are united to Christ in his suffering
for the salvation of the world.
Through our Lord Jesus Christ, your Son,
who lives and reigns with you
in the unity of the Holy Spirit,
one God, for ever and ever.

March 21, 2020 - In the midst of the coronavirus scare after the churches
had been closed for services, Bishop Strickland stood at the busiest
intersection in Tyler, Texas, blessing the people of God with the Real
Presence of Our Lord Jesus Christ in his Blessed Sacrament. He urged
every priest to do the same, to bring the Lord to his people!

**Rediscovering the spiritual treasures
that exist within the Eastern Catholic Churches**

The Church must breathe with her two lungs!
Unity in legitimate diversity.

—Pope St. John Paul II
Ut Unum Sint
May 25, 1995

It is earnestly recommended that Catholics avail themselves more
often of the spiritual treasures of the Eastern Fathers which lift up
the whole man to the contemplation of the divine mysteries.

—Pope St. John Paul II
Orientale Lumen
May 2, 1995

The Whole Church will esteem this "spiritual treasure"
(referring to the Eastern Catholic Churches)

—Pope Benedict XVI
Comments
November 4, 2011

Table of Contents

A Renewed Focus on Prayer

"Do not conform yourselves to this age but be transformed by the renewal of your mind, that you may discern what is the will of God, what is good and pleasing and perfect."
(Rom. 12:2)

"It is time for us to become a spiritual people again."
(Matthew Kelly)

Dear Fellow Pilgrim,

Based on the work we have done in the past decade, people we have met, and ministries we have undertaken, we have witnessed a profound spiritual hunger. One of the principle messages we have heard is that people want to know how to pray. This has been a consistent request from our youth to adults, and has also been reflected in parish surveys. Because prayer is an integral component of the spiritual life, we aim to provide some perspectives to fellow pilgrims who desire to deepen their relationship with Our Lord Jesus Christ, in order to cultivate a relationship with him and make him the center of their daily lives.

Herein, we focus on the Jesus Prayer, an ancient tradition with origins that can be traced back to the time of the Apostles. The oldest form of contemplative prayer, it developed, evolved, and has been faithfully practiced and preserved in the Eastern Churches, both Catholic and Orthodox, from post-Apostolic times to the present day. The Popes have recognized that this is one of the spiritual treasures that can be of great benefit to the Universal Catholic Church. As Pope St. John Paul II wrote, "It is earnestly recommended that Catholics avail themselves more often of the spiritual treasures of the Eastern Fathers which lift up the whole man to the contemplation of the divine mysteries."[1]

Because the Jesus Prayer is not as well known outside the Christian East, the reader will be introduced to certain concepts, such as *hesychia* and *nepsis*, which may be new. The reader also will be introduced to certain Spiritual Fathers with whom they are likely less familiar, but who are considered important figures in the development of the Jesus Prayer tradition. These will include St. Seraphim of Sarov, St. Ignatius Brianchaninov, Elder Porphyrios of Kavsokalyvia, St. Theophan the Recluse, and others. We believe that through a broadened awareness of our shared patrimony, these spiritual traditions can be a great source of inspiration and aid us in growth on the spiritual journey. We then discover or rediscover the beauty of our Catholic faith, which is ever ancient, ever new.

Since the second edition of this book, which was published in December 2015, the Church has been experiencing significant turmoil. We have seen statistics as to the epidemic departure in the United States of Catholics who currently identify themselves as "none" in terms of religious affiliation (the "nones" to whom Bishop Robert Barron refers).

Why are people disaffiliating from the Church? A comprehensive study done by St. Mary's Press from 2015-2017, published as *Going, Going, Gone: The Dynamics of Disaffiliation in Young Catholics,* provides some perspectives:

- Disillusionment and frustration that their questions about faith were not answered — nor were they given the opportunity to ask.

- Lack of companionship on the spiritual journey.

---

1   Pope St. John Paul II, *Orientale Lumen*, Apostolic Letter (Rome: Libreria Editrice Vaticana, May 2, 1995), no. 6.

- Struggles with difficult issues such as abortion, marriage, or contraception.[2]

Add to this that the spirit of the age has drifted significantly far afield of Gospel values and has created even greater questions and confusion. This includes the Obergefell decision[3] that challenges the sanctity of marriage and passage of laws supporting late-term abortion. As Archbishop Charles J. Chaput, OFM Cap of Philadelphia, described it, we are living in an increasingly post-Christian world.[4]

However, just as in the case of a devastating forest fire, new life emerges from the ashes. In 2019, we heard a number of influential people remind us of the importance of returning to prayer and our spiritual roots. His Eminence Robert Cardinal Sarah writes in his latest book, *The Day is Now Far Spent*, "The chief preoccupation of all disciples of Jesus must be their sanctification. The first place in their lives must be given to prayer, to silent contemplation, and to the Eucharist ..."[5] Catholic Apologist Matthew Kelly writes in his new book, *Rediscover the Saints*, "It is time for us to become a spiritual people again."[6] In the midst of the unfolding war for the salvation of souls, we concur that it is time to reprioritize prayer and, accordingly, we have decided to update our work in order to continue sharing contemplative prayer practices with our fellow sojourners.

There are many in the Church today who wonder what they can do in a time of turmoil. Some are tempted to leave. How can they make a difference? We remain convinced prayer is essential to the renewal of

---

2   Catholic News Service, "Young Adults Want to be Heard by the Church, Study Finds," *Texas Catholic Herald*, January 23 2018, 2. Reference is made to the survey contained in Robert J. McCarty and John M. Vitek, *Going, Going, Gone: The Dynamics of Disaffiliation in Young Catholics* (Winona, MN: St. Mary's Press, 2017). This survey was conducted from 2015-2017.

3   *Obergefell v. Hodges* (2015). Landmark civil rights case in which the United States Supreme Court ruled that the fundamental right to marry is guaranteed to same-sex couples.

4   See Charles J. Chaput, *Strangers in a Strange Land: Practicing the Catholic Faith in a Post-Christian World* (New York: Henry Holt, 2017).

5   Robert Cardinal Sarah, in conversation with Nicolas Diat, *The Day is Now Far Spent*, transl. Michael J. Miller (San Francisco, CA: Ignatius Press, 2019), 30.

6   Matthew Kelly, *Rediscover the Saints* (Assam, India: Blue Sparrow Books, 2019), 31.

3

the Church. Consider the example of Cardinal Ignatius Kung Pin-Mei (1901-2000), who spent 30 years in solitary confinement for refusing to compromise with the prevailing culture. He gave this advice in the face of hostility:

> Practice prayer, which is the most subversive of liberties; it can never be taken from you, and is a source of power and strength. Train yourself in prayer. Begin now, so that you are a fit, skilled practitioner when the need arises.[7]

Want to create radical action? Want to shake up our secular culture by refusing to give in? Want to renew the Church? Pray! Pray and trust that God has this situation in hand. Let prayer increase our love for God and strengthen our faith. For all these reasons, we hope this book will be of great benefit.

We have received overwhelmingly positive feedback from those who have been introduced to the Jesus Prayer through retreats, days of reflection, parish missions, and workshops that we have been delivering since 2011, both in the United States and in China. We have witnessed lives transformed through a renewed or deepened relationship with Christ. Especially gratifying is the response of our youth, who are the future of our Church. Thus, we have updated this book to support our efforts.

Readers will notice references to St. Teresa of Calcutta (Mother Teresa), a well-known contemporary figure who is living proof that a deep interior relationship with the Divine Presence can result in ordinary actions being transformed through extraordinary love. It is important to note, though, that Mother Teresa was not part of the Jesus Prayer tradition. In fact, while she herself had a deep prayer life and emphasized the importance of prayer to members of her Congregation, she did not teach a specific form of prayer. However,

---

7   See Elizabeth Scalia, "Exile: The Past is Prologue," *Patheos* (April 3, 2009).

from her writings we can conclude that her prayer reflected interior silence and prayer of the heart, both of which are essential components of the Jesus Prayer.

Mother Teresa had a "Simple Path" that was included on cards that she would hand out:

> The fruit of silence is prayer.
> The fruit of prayer is faith.
> The fruit of faith is love.
> The fruit of love is service.
> The fruit of service is peace.[8]

These thoughts would be equally at home in the Jesus Prayer tradition. For example, the prayer itself is grounded in silent contemplation.[9] Using the second fruit—faith—as an example, St. Ignatius Brianchaninov (1807-1867), a Spiritual Father within the Jesus Prayer tradition, wrote, "Constant prayer guides one to the acquisition of faith, because one who constantly prays begins gradually to sense the presence of God."[10] With respect to the third fruit—love—he added, "From all this, people begin to seem good, and from such a heart, love for one's fellow man usually arises."[11] Thus, with silence and prayer as the foundation, other fruits can be obtained that reflect love of God and, ultimately, manifested in love of neighbor, or service. In essence, the spiritual life is rooted in silent contemplation and prayer.

---

8   Cf. Mother Teresa, *A Simple Path,* comp. Lucinda Vardey (New York: Ballantine Books, 1995), 1. An Indian businessman and admirer of Mother Teresa printed cards with these five lines on yellow paper, which Mother Teresa regularly gave out and called her "business card."

9   We would be remiss in not mentioning Robert Cardinal Sarah's powerful work on this topic of silence: Robert Cardinal Sarah, in conversation with Nicolas Diat, *The Power of Silence: Against the Dictatorship of Noise,* transl. Michael J. Miller (San Francisco, CA: Ignatius Press, 2017).

10 Ignatius Brianchaninov, *The Refuge: Anchoring the Soul in God,* transl. Nicholas Kotar (Jordanville, NY: Holy Trinity Publications/The Printshop of St. Job of Pochaev, 2019), 30.

11 Ibid.

In a world in which many people find themselves searching for purpose and meaning, it is worth mentioning what is meant by this final fruit: peace. Some will immediately think world peace or something grandiose. However, this peace is even more profound. Jesus told his disciples, "Peace I leave with you; my peace I give to you. Not as the world gives do I give it to you. Do not let your hearts be troubled or afraid."[12]

The peace Jesus references is inner peace — peace and stillness within our souls. St. Ignatius Brianchaninov wrote:

> When the mind and heart unite in prayer and when the thoughts of the soul cease to wander, then the heart becomes warm with spiritual warmth, in which the light of Christ can shine, filling the inner man entirely with peace and joy.[13]

St. Seraphim of Sarov (1754-1833) said, "Learn to be peaceful and thousands around you will find salvation."[14] As St. Elizabeth of the Trinity (1880-1906) said in her well-known prayer: "O my God, Trinity whom I adore, help me to forget myself entirely that I may be established in you as still and as peaceful as if my soul were already in eternity."[15] This is the inner peace that Jesus gives, a foretaste of eternal blessedness in heaven.

This is the peace many seek, often without realizing it. Consider again the example of Mother Teresa. She had a deep-seated fire inside her, which radiated in her joy, her smile, and her energy to love Christ

---

12 John 14:27. All biblical quotes contained herein are from the NABRE 2011, unless otherwise specified.

13 St. Seraphim of Sarov, Instruction 11, "On Prayer." Cited in Brianchaninov, *The Refuge*, 187.

14 Valentine Zander, *St. Seraphim of Sarov,* transl. by Sister Gabriel Anne, SSC (Crestwood, NY: St. Vladimir's Seminary Press, 1975), x.

15 St. Elizabeth of the Trinity, OCD, *I Have Found God*, Complete Works, vol. 1, "Major Spiritual Writings," transl. Sr. Aletheia Kane, OCD (Washington, DC: ICS Publications, 2014), 183.

by recognizing his presence and serving him through the poorest of the poor. This peace as offered by Jesus is the antidote for the restless wandering of many. It is the antidote in times when the Christian faith and Gospel values are being challenged.

We hope that this focus on personal prayer will help readers round out their spiritual lives, the fullness of which includes both an interior relationship with the Divine and the sacramental life of the Church. These two are meant to go to together. One without the other leads to an incomplete spirituality. We hope that by discovering the strength gained through prayer, hearts will be ignited with love of God and his Church, which in turn forms spiritually vibrant people who, in turn, renew our parish communities, making them, too, spiritually vibrant.

Mother Teresa is proof that love of Jesus manifested in love for neighbor can transform the world. Those who knew her would describe her as an ordinary woman and of fragile health. Yet in 1985, UN Secretary General Javier Perez de Cuellar called her "the most powerful woman in the world." How does an elderly woman of ill health make such a profound impact on our world? Many people in interviews would ask Mother Teresa: What is your secret? How do you do what you do? Her answer was always the same: "My secret is simple … *I pray*."[16] Prayer was an incredibly important part of Mother Teresa's life; she had a very personal relationship with Jesus and she trusted him no matter what twists and turns, joys and disappointments she encountered in her life. No matter the challenges, her zeal never diminished. Prayer and, in turn, the encounter and relationship with Jesus, can truly set hearts afire.

At the outset, we also need to provide a disclaimer. The intention of this book is to expose readers to the Jesus Prayer and encourage adaption of its practices. However, it is only an introduction at best. Ongoing reading, the adoption of spiritual practices to cultivate the

---

16   Joseph Langford, MC, *Mother Teresa's Secret Fire: The Encounter that Changed Her Life and How It Can Transform Your Own* (Huntington, IN: Our Sunday Visitor Publishing Division, 2008), 175.

correct environment for prayer, and spiritual guidance[17] all should be considered as the spiritual journey unfolds. It is our desire to plant the seed, realizing ongoing cultivation and nurturing is required for the seed to germinate, develop deep roots, and bear lasting fruit. Consider this book a first fertilization after the seed has been planted.

Consider, too, this analogy. Assume a person decides to train for a marathon. He or she might attend a preparatory course in which the instructor provides an overview of the importance of stretching techniques. The participant even practices the techniques in class and seems to understand them. However, when he or she goes home and continues the techniques, questions arise: "Is this the right way? That does not feel right." The instructor is not there to answer questions, so doubt and confusion begin to set in. Soon, the person may become discouraged and give up: "I can't do this. I never should have thought I could run a marathon."

Now, consider a person who attended a parish mission, listened to a 45-minute conference on the Jesus Prayer, spent 20 minutes in silence practicing the techniques of the prayer, actually had a good experience, and continues practicing the prayer post-retreat at home. However, questions set in, followed by doubts, and this person, too, gives up. "I can't do this!"

The purpose of this book is to bridge the gap from a retreat or conference through the questions that will arise afterward, and through the insights gained herein, help the person conclude, "I can do this!" rather than give up in despair. Again, this is not intended for the entire spiritual journey where much more cultivation is required. Rather, it is the first fertilization, the boost needed not to give up.

---

17   An article worth considering in this regard is Elizabeth Anderson, "How Spiritual Direction Transformed a Catholic High School," *National Catholic Reporter* online (February 6, 2019). The high school reported that over 20 young men had entered the seminary after spiritual direction was introduced six years earlier. This practice was offered in response to the question raised by students of "Where do we go from here?" after experiencing a spiritual high point on a retreat. Consider this in light of the reason many young people disaffiliate with the Church: lack of companionship on the spiritual journey.

This book is meant to be a reference guide, with each chapter standing on its own and providing specific information. For example, if someone is interested in the importance of prayer, then Chapter 1 is most relevant. A brief historical development of the Jesus Prayer is in Chapter 2 and the technique in Chapter 3. Most readers likely will have questions about the Prayer, which is the intention of Chapter 4 with questions and answers outlined. Some may be interested in what is next and how the Jesus Prayer fits into the broader Art of Spiritual Life, which is included in Chapter 5. Finally, there is supplemental information: A historical timeline, glossary of key terms, and additional recommended reading. Accordingly, the reader does not have to start at the beginning; he or she can go to the section of most interest.

Prayer is hard work. However, it can deepen our relationship with the Risen Lord, making it personal and creating the foundation for growth on the spiritual journey. Knowing the Risen Lord will help us discern our true propose in life, which is eternal blessedness, living in union with God. May all of us be renewed and experience our deepest yearnings fulfilled by entering more deeply into relationship with the Divine Presence that dwells in every human heart (see Luke 17:21).

It is also our fervent hope that this book can, in some small way, support the efforts of His Grace Bishop Milan Lach, SJ of the Eparchy in Parma in his call to his people for spiritual renewal as outlined in his 2019 pastoral letter for the Feast of the Theophany.[18] As he previously stated, one of his priorities as a bishop is to teach people how to pray.

For each of us, the pilgrim journey continues ...

Let your love for God change the world,
but never let the world change your love for God.

---

18   See Bishop Milan Lach, SJ. "A Year of Renewal." Pastoral Letter to the Faithful of the Byzantine Catholic Eparchy of Parma (January 6, 2019).

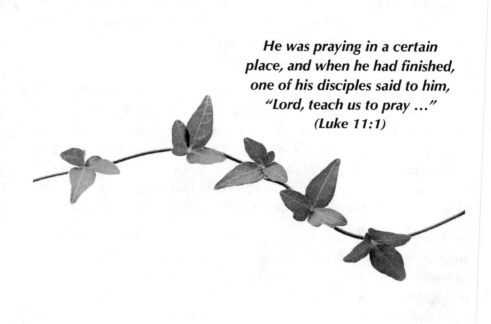

He was praying in a certain place, and when he had finished, one of his disciples said to him, "Lord, teach us to pray ..."
(Luke 11:1)

CHAPTER 1

The Quest for Purpose

"Man seeks joy and happiness in heaven. He seeks what is eternal
from everyone and everything. He seeks to find joy in God. God is
a mystery. He is silence. He is infinite. He is everything. Everyone
possess this inclination of the soul to heaven. All people seek something
heavenly. All beings turn toward him, albeit unconsciously."[19]
(Elder Porphyrios of Kavsokalyvia)

"The invincible desire of every man is holiness. God himself
implanted in the heart of man this unceasing divine yearning"[20]
(Monk Moses of Mount Athos)

Opening Scripture Reading

Read: Rev. 3:14-21 (Behold, I stand at the door and knock).

Our Souls Thirst for the Living God

It is hard not to notice the darkness, despair, pessimism, and polarization that has permeated our American culture. We all thirst for meaning and purpose in our lives. Many seek, often in vain. Some recognize it is God whom they seek ("My soul thirsts for God, the Living God."[21]). To exacerbate the situation, secular society provides us with "advice" and quick answers as to what will fill that

---

19 Elder Porphyrios, *Wounded by Love: The Life and Wisdom of Elder Porphyrios*, ed. Sisters of the Holy Convent of Chrysopigi, transl. John Raffan (Limni, Evia, Greece: Denise Harvey, 2013), 113.

20 Monk Moses of Mount Athos, *Holiness: Is It Attainable Today?*, transl. Fr. Peter A. Chamberas (Brookline, MA: Holy Cross Orthodox Press, 2012), 8.

21 Psalm 42:3.

inner sense of longing or search for purpose, much of which leads to greater emptiness, despair, disillusionment, and negativity. The cure offered by the world is never as advertised or wears off all too quickly.

Here is the reality: Only God can truly satisfy our innermost longing. Only God is truly inexhaustible. One author writes: "We seek for something or someone else to [quench] our inner thirst, to fill the void God created as a sacred place for himself, a void large enough that only he can fill."[22] God created us for one purpose and one purpose alone, to share his overwhelming love. Until we surrender ourselves and allow him to fill our hearts completely, we will never experience true human fulfillment—there will always be something missing. There also seems to be a correlation: the farther we are away from God, the deeper the longing within.

Early Greek Father St. Gregory of Nyssa (335-395) actually wrote about this, calling it the experience of our own dissatisfaction. He tells us that we can have all the food, honors, personal recognition, power, praise, sexual intimacy, or other pleasures that we seek, and somehow, we will still find ourselves empty. The feeling of fulfillment is only temporary and, in the end, we remain dissatisfied. So, Gregory concludes that either we are the most pitiable of creatures, seeking for something that does not exist, or there is something that transcends time and space that can truly fill our deepest longing. That something, he concludes, is God.

We find ourselves in a world of increasing darkness, where God is no longer a priority in our lives. Yet, the Gospel provides us with Good News that is an antidote to the current malaise: *God wants a personal, intimate relationship with us*—each of us, no matter where we have been on our life journey or what darkness we have experienced. The same God who created the universe, the God who is "ineffable, inconceivable, invisible, incomprehensible,

---

22   Langford, *Mother Teresa's Secret Fire*, 191.

ever-existing, yet ever the same,"[23] a God beyond all our imagining, desires to be in relationship with us. Our deepest longing can be fulfilled only by establishing a personal, intimate relationship with him.[24] This is God as Jesus has revealed him to us, a God who cares so much for us that even the very hairs on our head have been counted.[25]

God is not "out there somewhere" or inaccessible to us. He is not a concept, ideal, or hypothesis.[26] God in his essence is relational, reflected in the Trinitarian relationship among the three Divine Persons. He is closer to us than we can imagine—he is within us—and we can experience his presence, if we are attuned to it. God loves us and wants us to love him back. We cannot have a relationship with a concept. God is personal, and it is his greatest desire to draw near to us and accompany us on our journey in life, wherein our true destiny is eternal blessedness and union with him.

Only God is inexhaustible; his goodness, love, mercy, compassion, and patience are without measure. Everything else falls short. Money runs out, we lose energy in our pursuits, the thrills no longer have the same effect, relationships run dry, we have accomplished our goals, reputation can be lost in an instant, and our family and friends have come and gone. Yet, God remains ever the same, ever constant, ever present, and ever faithful. As St. Teresa of Ávila (1515-1582) wrote:

> Let nothing disturb you. Let nothing frighten you. All
> things are passing away. God never changes. Patience

---

23 From the Anaphora (consecration prayer) of the Divine of Liturgy of St. John Chrysostom. *The Divine Liturgies of Our Holy Father John Chrysostom* (Pittsburgh: Byzantine Seminary Press, 2006), 72.

24 See Eph. 1:5–6. The God and Father of our Lord Jesus Christ "destined us for adoption to himself through Jesus Christ, in accord with the favor of his will, for the praise of the glory of his grace that he granted us in the beloved."

25 See Matt. 10:30.

26 See Archbishop Charles J. Chaput, OFM Cap., *Living the Catholic Faith: Rediscovering the Basics* (Cincinnati, OH: St. Anthony Messenger Press, 2001), 17.

obtains all things. Whoever has God lacks nothing. God alone is enough.[27]

God never gives up on us. He knocks at the door of our hearts[28] and "he will not rest until he has moved us from the gutter to the Palace."[29] He proved his love for us by sending us his Son, Jesus Christ, who lived, died, and rose from the dead, so that we too could have eternal life. This is the Good News of the Gospel. Jesus is God's personal invitation to us.[30] He has revealed God to us, his love for us, and how to attain the eternal life that God wants to give us. More importantly, Jesus gave us the example of how to live in relationship with God in order to fulfill our destiny. Further, Jesus is not simply a historical figure, come and gone. Jesus is alive and we can continue to experience him, to enter into relationship with him. One cannot have a meaningful relationship with a dead historical figure.

How do we fill our deepest longing? How do we discover purpose and meaning in our lives? Pope Francis wrote in *Evangelii Gaudium*, "The Joy of the Gospel fills the hearts and lives of all who *encounter* Jesus."[31] He adds, "Those who accept his offer of salvation are set free from sin, sorrow, inner emptiness and loneliness."[32] For many of us, this is exactly what we are seeking: an escape from our inner emptiness and loneliness, from the constant, fruitless search for meaning, or looking for love in all the wrong places. This Joy of the Gospel is the abundant life that Jesus said he came to bring,[33]

---

27 "Prayer of St. Teresa of Ávila." See www.ewtn.com/Devotionals/prayers/StTeresaofAvila.htm. Recall our previous discussion on interior peace, the peace given by Jesus and which the world cannot give.

28 See Rev. 3:20. See also John 15:23.

29 Anthony M. Coniaris, *Tools for Theosis: Becoming God-like in Christ* (Minneapolis: Light & Life Publishing Company, 2014), 80.

30 See Heb. 1:1-2. "In times past, God spoke in partial and various ways to our ancestors through the prophets; in these last days, he spoke to us through a son, whom he made heir of all things and through whom he created the universe."

31 Pope Francis, *Evangelii Gaudium*, Apostolic Exhortation (Rome: Libreria Editrice Vaticana, Nov. 24, 2013), no. 1. Emphasis added by the author.

32 Ibid.

33 See John 10:10b: "I came so that they might have life and have it more abundantly."

the one the Father desires to give us. By encountering the Divine Presence that dwells within, our lives can be truly transformed. Thus, the experience of authentic joy begins by encountering Jesus Christ.

Cultivating a Relationship with Jesus

Consider all the great saints we know. Think about their great faith; reflect on the fire that burned within each of them. Consider such people as Mother Teresa. Consider some of the great conversion stories such as that of St. Augustine of Hippo (354-430), who wrote about his search for meaning in his *Confessions*.[34] A modern-day equivalent of radical conversion might be Dorothy Day of New York, who describes her coming to faith (*The Long Loneliness*). Consider everyday people we know who have made significant contributions to society or the Church, or endured incredible hardships with grace. How did they gain such incredible faith?

While the seed of faith is implanted in each of us at our Baptism, it requires effort to cultivate that seed, enabling it to develop deep roots and bear abundant fruit. Even if a person has a great conversion event, including tragedy or encounter, that spark of faith requires ongoing nurturing. So, how does one find such strong faith?

Mother Teresa's Simple Path actually provides us with a good overview.

---

34 If one is interested in reading the *Confessions*, there are numerous translations. Highly recommended is St. Augustine of Hippo, *Confessions*, transl. Henry Chadwick (NY: Oxford University Press, 2009).

The fruit of silence is prayer.	• God comes to us in the silent recesses of our heart, a heart that is open to him. • In silence, we learn to encounter him in prayer (the topic discussed herein).
The fruit of prayer is faith.	• By entering into relationship with God, we learn to trust him; to know that he has our best interests at heart.
The fruit of faith is love.	• The deeper our relationship with God, the greater our love for him. We learn to love with all our heart, our whole soul, our whole mind, and our whole strength.[35] • Our love for God is, in turn, manifested in our love of neighbor, recognizing that we are all children of God.

---

35   See Luke 10:27.

The fruit of love is service.	• Love of God and neighbor often manifests itself in service, recognizing that we all are members of one body, one Body in Christ.[36]
The fruit of service is peace.	• The fruit of our service can have significant impact, it is transformational. • We begin to experience the peace Jesus came to bring, the peace the world cannot give.[37] This is a deep inner peace. • As St. Irenaeus of Lyons wrote, "The glory of God is man fully alive."

What the table above illustrates is that a deep faith does not just happen. It originates in silence and when one enters into relationship with God through his Son Jesus Christ. Prayer is a primary means by which we nurture this relationship, encountering the Divine Presence in a very real, very personal way.

Cardinal Sarah wrote:

> Faith grows in an intense life of prayer and contemplative silence. It is nourished and strengthened in a daily face-to-face meeting with God and in an attitude of adoration and silent contemplation. It is professed

36   See Rom. 12:5.
37   See John 14:27.

in the Creed, celebrated in the liturgy, lived out in keeping the Commandments. It achieves its growth through an interior life of adoration and prayer. Faith is nourished by the liturgy, by Catholic doctrine, and by the Church's tradition as a whole. Its principal sources are Sacred Scripture, the Fathers of the Church, and the Magisterium.[38]

Thus, the foundation of the spiritual life begins with contemplative silence, which ultimately underpins a strong faith, nurtured through prayer and the sacramental life of the Church. In essence, this is the base for The Art of Spiritual Life. We begin in silence, which is the proper environment for an encounter.

Encountering the Risen Jesus

What is an encounter with Jesus like? We have only to turn to the Gospel for answers. One notable encounter is the two disciples who meet the Risen Lord on the road to Emmaus.[39] Consider for a moment their disposition: they are likely depressed and dejected over the crucifixion and death of Jesus, discussing how they had hoped he would have been "the one." Their departure from Jerusalem indicates their level of pessimism about the future, and one can sense from the words of Sacred Scripture how deeply defeated they felt, both emotionally and spiritually. Yet once they recognize Jesus in the breaking of the bread, what happens? They say to one another, *"Were not our hearts burning within us?"*[40] Not only did they have this intense interior feeling, they also felt compelled to do something about it. Despite the long journey that day and despite having already settled into their lodging for the evening, they immediately retraced their steps to Jerusalem with new-found energy to report what they

---

38   Robert Cardinal Sarah, *The Day is Now Far Spent,* 26.
39   See Luke 24:13-15.
40   Luke 24.32.

had experienced. One can imagine the enthusiasm of their report: *"The Lord has truly been raised!"* That is what it is like when a heart has experienced the Living Jesus—a heart enkindled with fire. Such an encounter is so overwhelming that the two disciples could not contain their joy; they simply had to share it.[41]

Where do we find Jesus today? We only have to look into the human heart to find him. Mother Teresa would tell us: "Don't search for Jesus in far lands; he is not there. He is close to you; he is in you."[42] Some believe that the idea of having a personal encounter with Jesus Christ is a Protestant phenomenon or something New Age. Yet nothing could be further from the truth! The idea of having a personal encounter with the Son of God goes back to the most ancient times of the Church, back to the Apostles and back to the Desert Fathers and Mothers who, beginning in the third century, withdrew to the Egyptian Deserts to seek the presence of God. They understood that encountering the Divine Presence of Jesus dwelling within them was done within the human heart. This encounter is an important dimension for realizing the fullness of the spiritual life, the abundant life Jesus came to bring.[43]

The Fullness of the Spiritual Life

The fullness of the spiritual life was always intended to consist of two components: (1) an intense personal, interior prayer relationship with Jesus Christ, to experience the Divine Presence, and (2) the sacramental life of the Church, to experience his presence in the sacraments, and being united with a body of believers who are also seeking to have their lives transformed by encountering Jesus. These two components were never intended to be separated. Consider for

---

41 See Pope St. John Paul II, *Novo Millennio Ineunte* (Rome: Libreria Editrice Vaticana, 2001), no. 40. "Those who have had genuine contact with Christ cannot keep him to themselves; they must proclaim him."

42 See also Luke 17:21. "The kingdom of God is within you" (Orthodox Study Bible).

43 See John 10:10.

a moment how much more meaning it has to receive Jesus in the Eucharist when one has a personal encounter with him cultivated through prayer. We have a genuine longing for his presence in our midst, longing to receive him in the sacrament. Think of how much more powerful the words heard in Confession, "Your sins are forgiven," are when one has an interior relationship with Jesus. We are drawn to him to experience healing in the sacrament. It is personal. When we hear the words of Sacred Scripture in the liturgy along with the homily, we find new meaning and beauty because of our interior relationship. The Lenten practices of fasting and almsgiving take on new meaning when Jesus Christ is the center of one's life. All for Jesus, only Jesus. We are drawn to a deeper interior conversion (*metanoia*) because of our genuine desire to be in relationship with God. Thus, the interior relationship formed in prayer and the sacramental life of the Church truly complement one another.

The Crisis of Faith we are experiencing today, particularly in the United States and Western Europe, is not because structured religion has lost meaning, as some like to argue. The crisis exists because many have lost or have not been exposed to one of the most fundamental components of the spiritual life: the ability to encounter Jesus through prayer. Simply put, we as a Church and a society no longer know how to pray as we should.[44] Beginning with Pope Benedict XVI's declaration of the Church's Year of Faith (October 11, 2012–November 24, 2013)[45] and reinforced by Pope Francis in his Apostolic Exhortation, *Evangelii Gaudium*, we are encouraged to seek a deeper encounter with the living Jesus. Accordingly, we will focus on the encounter with Jesus through the experience of personal prayer, which brings us back to the fullness of the spiritual life.

---

44 Cf. Gabriel Bunge, OSB, *Earthen Vessels: The Practice of Personal Prayer According to the Patristic Tradition* (San Francisco: Ignatius Press, 2002), 9. This Swiss Benedictine monk describes the "evaporation of faith" and how, despite best efforts, Christianity seems to be growing cold. His premise is that somehow, we have lost touch with the importance of a personal prayer life which was always an essential part of the mystical tradition of the Early Church.

45 See Benedict XVI, *Porta Fidei* (*The Door of Faith*), Apostolic Letter (Rome: Libreria Editrice Vaticana, Oct. 11, 2012).

The Art of Spiritual Life is intended to recreate spiritual disciplines, the basics, to recognize the longing for God in our lives. An essential component is learning to pray, as well as creating the right environment for prayer through practices such as fasting and almsgiving. We will explore this further in Chapter 5.

It is Jesus Whom We Seek

Take a moment to consider Jesus's encounter with the paralytic at the Pool of Siloam.[46] He has been lying by the pool for 38 years because there is a system ("the angel comes to stir the waters"[47]) and the system fails him ("someone else always gets down there before me"[48]). "I have no one,"[49] the paralytic laments to Jesus. How many of us are like the paralytic, lying on our mats, weighed down by the burdens of life or doubt or despair, believing there is no one?[50]

Yet Jesus is *someone*. He comes to us; he came to us in our humanity and will walk with us if we desire his accompaniment. He will heal us, not having to work any system. If Jesus is at the center of our lives, healing is guaranteed in this life or the next. Further, Jesus tells the man, "Rise, take up your mat, and walk."[51] Jesus does not take away our burdens or earthly trials. However, rather than be paralyzed by them, we are given by Jesus the ability to lift and carry them. This is the person for whom so many of us thirst. He will remain with us on the journey and never leave our hearts, helping us bear our burdens and guiding us to eternal blessedness as promised us by Our Loving Father. We simply need to allow him to enter our hearts and our lives.

---

46   See John 5:1-15.
47   John 5:4.
48   John 5:7.
49   John 5:7.
50   The Fourth Sunday of Easter in the Eastern Churches is the Sunday of the Paralytic. The Kontakion for this Sunday is: "By your divine intercession, O Lord, as you raised up the paralytic of old, so raise up my soul, paralyzed by sins and thoughtless acts, so that being saved I may sing to you: 'Glory to your Power, O Compassionate Christ!'"
51   John 5:8.

Jesus Thirsts for Us

We thirst for Jesus; he thirsts for us too. Among Jesus's final words on the cross were, "I thirst."[52] He thirsts for our love and for our souls. As Mother Teresa tells us: "Until you know deep inside that Jesus thirsts for you—you cannot begin to know who he wants to be for you. Or who he wants you to be for him."[53] Jesus stands at the door of our hearts right now and knocks.[54] Do we hear him? Do we have the courage to answer? Will we let him in? He comes to console us, strengthen us, to lift us up, and bind our wounds. He comes to dispel our darkness and doubts. He desires to transform our lives so that we can attain the abundant life. Jesus knows our hearts; he accepts us exactly as we are.[55] He desires to make his dwelling within us.[56] Will we let him enter our hearts?[57]

Many of us thirst; we want to fill the inner longing that exists in our lives.[58] We want to be set free from sorrow, inner emptiness and loneliness. Yet only God can truly fill this longing.[59] If we seek elsewhere, we find too many things we *think* will satisfy the thirst—but none really do. In our innermost depths, our souls thirst for the Living God[60]—whether we realize it or not. How many of us are slowly dying of thirst without realizing it, burdened down by earthly cares? Elder Porphyrios of Kavsokalyvia (1906-91) said, "When people are empty of Christ, a thousand and one other things come and fill them up: jealousies, hatreds, boredom, melancholy, resentment, a worldly

---

52   John 19:28.

53   Mother Teresa, *Come Be My Light: The Private Writings of the 'Saint of Calcutta,'* Edited and with commentary by Brian Kolodiejchuk, MC (New York: Doubleday, 2007), 42.

54   See Rev. 3:20.

55   See Langford, *Mother Teresa's Secret* Fire, 133-134.

56   See John 14:23.

57   Pope Benedict XVI, *Porta Fidei,* no. 10. "Saint Luke teaches that knowing the content (of faith) to be believed is not sufficient unless the heart, the authentic sacred space within the person, is opened by grace that allows the eyes to see below the surface and to understand that what has been proclaimed is the word of God."

58   Pope Benedict XVI, *Porta Fidei,* no.13. "In (Jesus Christ), all the anguish and all the longing of the human heart finds fulfillment."

59   See Langford, 191.

60   See Psalm 42:2-3.

outlook, worldly pleasures. Try to fill your soul with Christ so that it's not empty."[61]

Why are we unwilling to open the doors of our hearts to Jesus, who patiently knocks and waits? Are we too afraid of self-surrender or trusting that Jesus has our best interests at heart? Are we ashamed of our past? Are we distracted by the attractive packaging, the bows and the ribbons, the marketing blitz, and the empty promises offered to us by secular society? Are we discouraged by others, made to feel embarrassed to rely on our faith? Why do we hesitate? "Christ stands outside the door of our soul and knocks for us to open to him, but uninvited, he does not enter. He doesn't want to violate the freedom he himself gave us."[62]

Jesus thirsts for us, he longs for us. We are each precious to him— *just as we are.* Let us set aside all our earthly cares and open the doors of our hearts to him. Let us listen to the words we long to hear: *I love you! You are forgiven!*

The Importance of Church (the Body of Christ)

The fullness of the spiritual life includes the sacramental life of the Church, which is another means of encountering Jesus. Experiencing Jesus in personal prayer, recognizing the Divine Presence within, provides an even deeper meaning to our sacramental encounters. They were always meant to go together. Further, Jesus tells us that where two or three are gathered in his name, he is in their midst.[63] Thus, we gather as a community because one separated from the other will leave us incomplete.

Unfortunately, many people today describe themselves as "spiritual," but reject the notion of an institutionalized Church. They believe spirituality and a transcendent purpose are something

---

61 Elder Porphyrios, *Wounded by Love*, 177.
62 Ibid., 109.
63 Cf. Matt. 18:20.

to be pursued individually. Yet as Sr. Sandra M. Schneiders, IHM, a foremost authority on spirituality, argues, the spiritual traditions of the Church are precisely what we need to understand our spiritual-life experiences.[64] We receive our life-giving spiritual tradition *through* the institutionalized Church, the Christian tradition centered in Jesus Christ and which has been institutionalized in the Roman and Eastern Catholic Churches.[65] Divorcing the spiritual life from the Church, as Sr. Schneiders wrote, "Is a classic case of curing a headache by decapitation."[66] The spiritual traditions are handed onto us by the Church, and we need these spiritual traditions to understand, guide, and support our encounters with Jesus, who is the source of life. Thus, we can never separate our growth in the spiritual life from the Church. They are indelibly linked.

We also need to consider the Church in the context of the Body of Christ. All are members of this Body because all are created in the Divine Image.[67] Jesus tells us, "I am the vine, you are the branches."[68] All of us are connected together through a common source of life, with Christ, who is the Head of the Body.[69] St. Paul wrote, "So we, though many, are one body in Christ and individually parts of one another."[70] Mother Teresa would tell us that if a single drop of water was missing from the ocean, the entire ocean would be impoverished because of the missing drop. Pope Francis wrote, "Loving others is a spiritual force drawing us to union with God."[71] Thus, we seek the well-being of all members of the Body of Christ so that the value of the whole, our own value, is not diminished. As Elder Porphyrios wrote:

---

64 See Sandra M. Schneiders, "Religion vs. Spirituality: A Contemporary Conundrum," *Spiritus: A Journal of Christian Spirituality* 3/2 (2003), 169.
65 Ibid. 171.
66 Ibid.
67 See Gen 1:26-27.
68 John 15:5
69 See Col. 1:18.
70 Rom. 12:5.
71 Pope Francis, *Evangelii Gaudium*, no. 272.

The important thing is for us to enter into the Church—
to unite ourselves with our fellow men, with the joys
and sorrows of each and every one, to feel that they
are our own, to pray for everyone, to have care for their
salvation, to forget about ourselves, to do everything
for them just as Christ did for us. In the Church we
become one with the unfortunate, suffering, and
sinful soul.[72]

Pope Francis also speaks about spiritual accompaniment, about humbly supporting one another on the journey. He describes it as "removing our sandals before the sacred ground of others," walking with each other "in a steady and reassuring manner, reflecting our closeness and a compassionate gaze that heals, liberates, and encourages our growth in the Christian life."[73] We truly are in this together.

Finally, hearts that encounter Jesus are prompted to action. Consider Zacchaeus, the chief tax collector, and his profound conversion experience (*metanoia*), giving away his wealth and making restitution to those whom he defrauded.[74] Think of Mary Magdalene weeping at the tomb. When she encounters the Risen Jesus, she immediately goes to the apostles to proclaim the Resurrection.[75] Consider Paul and his encounter with Jesus on the road to Damascus,[76] transformed from persecuting the Church of Christ to becoming one of its greatest missionaries and evangelists. Encounters with Jesus transform lives and stir hearts. An interior love for God will manifest itself in love of neighbor ("the fruit of faith is love"). Jesus tells us the two commandments of love of God and love of neighbor are indelibly linked.[77] As St. John Chrysostom would tell us: If we cannot recognize

---

72   Elder Porphyrios, *Wounded by Love*, 89.
73   Pope Francis, *Evangelii Gaudium*, no. 169-170.
74   See Luke 19:1-10
75   See John 20:11-18.
76   See Acts 9:1-9.
77   See Matt. 22:36-40.

Christ in the beggar at the church door, we cannot recognize him in the Eucharist, either.[78]

The Importance of Personal Prayer in Encountering Jesus

In his ministry, Jesus emphasized the importance of an interior conversion of heart. A major theme of his message was repentance, with the opening proclamation of his ministry being, "Repent, the kingdom of heaven is at hand."[79] As he tells the Pharisees, "Cleanse first the inside of the cup, so that the outside also may be clean."[80] In the Parable of the Sower,[81] Jesus describes the condition of the soil required for the seed to bear fruit, the seed being the word of God and the soil being the interior condition of the one who responds.[82] In the Parable of the Good Samaritan,[83] Jesus reverses the position of neighbor as being one of legal obligation (who deserves my love?) to one of self-giving (I freely choose to show myself as neighbor to others in need).[84] We are called to forgive one another from the heart.[85] Jesus shatters the narrowness of our hearts, essentially saying if we love God with our whole heart, we will love others as well, without restrictions or limitations, even our enemies and those who persecute us.[86] If we fail in this regard, St. John the Evangelist calls us out: "If anyone says, 'I love God,' but hates his brother, he is a liar; for whoever does not love a brother whom he has seen cannot love God whom he has not seen."[87]

---

78   Cf. St. John Chrysostom. "If you cannot find Christ in the beggar at the church door, you will not find him in the chalice."

79   Matt. 3:2. He makes this same proclamation again in Matt. 4:17. In Mark 1:15c, the message is "Repent, and believe in the Gospel." When Jesus commissions the twelve, "they went off and preached repentance" (Mark 6:12).

80   Cf. Matt. 23:26.

81   See Matt. 13:3-9.

82   See Matt. 13:18-23.

83   See Luke 10:25-37.

84   Luke Timothy Johnson, *The Gospel of Luke*. Taken from the Sacra Pagina series, vol. 3, ed. Daniel J. Harrington, SJ (Collegeville, MN: The Liturgical Press, 1991), 173.

85   See Matt. 18:35.

86   See Matt. 5:44.

87   1 John 4:20.

Ultimately, we will be judged on how we treated the least among us, for what we did for them we did for Christ.[88] This is Mother Teresa's Gospel on Five Fingers.[89] Thus, we are brought back to our solidarity within the Body of Christ. We are called to a deeper relationship with God and, in turn, our love for God manifests itself in love for neighbor. This love for God, this relationship with him, begins to create an interior change away from self-centeredness, selfishness, pride, and all that prevents our hearts from rising to God and loving as we should.

The kingdom of God is a spiritual reality present within the Christian believer and within the community of the Church. Our actions of love, mercy, compassion, and self-surrender to the will of God should be based on a purified heart (cleansing the inside of the cup first). Thus, the personal encounter with Jesus in prayer, cultivating a relationship with him and recognizing the Divine Presence, is how our hearts are initially transformed to live the lives to which God calls us. The more we recognize the Divine Presence within ourselves, the more we begin to recognize the Divine Presence in others, which draws us to love and unites us as the Body of Christ. As Pope Francis wrote, mercy is "the bridge that connects God and man, opening our hearts to a hope of being loved forever despite our sinfulness."[90]

How do we encounter the Living Jesus? One important way is in personal prayer, in the silent recesses of our heart. Specifically, we need contemplative prayer to listen to the voice of Jesus within the depths of our hearts, to revitalize our hearts and hear his knocking so to let him in. If we want to personally encounter Jesus, contemplative

---

88 See Matt. 25:31-46.
89 See Leo Maasburg, *Mother Teresa of Calcutta: A Personal Portrait*, trans. Michael J. Miller (San Francisco: Ignatius Press, 2010), 36. "Mother Teresa sometimes held up five fingers of one hand to explain this. The whole Gospel, she said, could be counted on five fingers: 'You-did-it-to-me!'" She references Matt. 25:40. In a letter dated June 1990, Mother Teresa tells her congregation "Remember the five fingers—you-did-it-to Me." See Mother Teresa, *Come Be My Light: The Private Writings of the Saint of Calcutta*, ed. Brian Kolodiejchuk (New York: Doubleday, 2007), 314.
90 Pope Francis, *Misericordiae Vultus (The Face of Mercy)*, Papal Bull (Rome: Libreria Editrice Vaticana, Apr. 11, 2015), no. 2.

prayer is one of the ways. Such prayer has two critical components: (1) praying from the heart and (2) interior silence. The most ancient form of such contemplative prayer is the Jesus Prayer. Recent popes have encouraged us to rediscover the spiritual treasures of the Eastern Catholic Churches, the Jesus Prayer being one part of this rich mystical tradition, faithfully preserved and practiced since shortly after the time of Christ on earth.

"I invite all Christians, everywhere, at this very moment,
to a renewed personal encounter with Jesus Christ,
or at least an openness to let him enter them; I ask
all of you to do this unfailingly every day."[91]

—*Pope Francis*

Without me you can do nothing.
(John 15:5)

---

91   Pope Francis, *Evangelii Gaudium*, no. 3.

CHAPTER 2

Seeking Silence and Solitude

"... but he would withdraw to deserted places to pray."
(Luke 5:16)

"Learn to love prayer. In order not to live in darkness, turn on the switch of prayer so that divine light may flood your soul. Christ will appear in the depths of your being. There, in the deepest and most inward part, is the Kingdom of God. The Kingdom of God is within you."[92]
(Elder Porphyrios of Kavsokalyvia)

"We encounter God only in the eternal silence in which he abides."[93]
(Robert Cardinal Sarah)

Opening Gospel Passage

Read: Luke 5:12-16 (Jesus cleanses the leper).

Jesus Himself Provides the Example of Personal Prayer

We are in urgent need of silence. With the busyness of our lives, it is hard to slow down and take time for Jesus. Yet, whether we realize it or not, we need Jesus more than we need food, water, light, or life itself. Silence becomes a foundation upon which our faith is ultimately built.

Jesus himself reinforced the importance of personal prayer and often withdrew to spend time with his Father. Prior to beginning his

---

92   Elder Porphyrios, *Wounded by Love*, 113.
93   Robert Cardinal Sarah, *The Power of Silence*, 21.

earthly ministry, Jesus spent 40 days in the desert to pray. Before he taught, preached, or healed, we often hear how he went off to a secluded place to pray. Why did Jesus originally go up Mount Tabor, where he was transfigured? Luke tells us that he went up the mountain to pray.[94] Also in the Gospel of Luke, Jesus tells His disciples the Parable of the Persistent Widow.[95] It begins: "And he told them a parable about the necessity to pray always without becoming weary."[96] Jesus prayed and he encouraged his disciples to pray. As one noted scripture scholar observed, "Prayer is a constant motif in Luke-Acts, and the critical moments of Jesus's ministry are punctuated by prayer."[97] Here is a brief overview of the importance of prayer in Jesus's life.

Passages from the Gospel of Luke	Event
After all the people had been baptized and Jesus also had been baptized and was **praying**, heaven was opened and the Holy Spirit descended upon him in bodily form like a dove. And a voice came from heaven, "You are my beloved Son; with you I am well pleased." (Luke 3:21-22).	Ministry begins in prayer, with receipt of the Holy Spirit
The report about him spread all the more, and great crowds assembled to listen to him and to be cured of their ailments, but he would withdraw to deserted places to **pray**. (Luke 5:15-16).	Solitude and Prayer
In those days he departed to the mountain to **pray**, and he spent the night in prayer to God. (Luke 6:12).	Solitude and Prayer

---

94 Luke 9:28.
95 See Luke 18:1-8.
96 Luke 18:1.
97 Johnson, *The Gospel of Luke*, 69.

Passages from the Gospel of Luke	Event
Once when Jesus **was praying** in solitude, and the disciples were with him, he asked them, "Who do the crowds say that I am?" (Luke 9:18).	Solitude and Prayer
About eight days after he said this, he took Peter, John, and James and went up the mountain **to pray**. (Luke 9:28)	Solitude and Prayer
While he **was praying** his face changed in appearance and his clothing became dazzling white. (Luke 9:29).	Prayer and Transformation
He **was praying** in a certain place, and when he had finished, one of his disciples said to him, "Lord, teach us to pray just as John taught his disciples." (Luke 11:1).	Time in prayer; teaching others to pray
He was in such agony and he **prayed** so fervently that his sweat became like drops of blood falling on the ground. (Luke 22:41).	Prayer in time of distress
When he rose from **prayer** and returned to his disciples, he found them sleeping from grief. (Luke 22:45).	Prayer in time of distress
He said to them, "Why are you sleeping? Get up and **pray** that you may not undergo the test." (Luke 22:46).	Prayer in time of trial

From this, we see a clear theme of Jesus spending time in prayer, often in solitude. He illustrated that prayer is "essential to the response of faith."[98] In addition, Jesus called God "My Father," with the underlying Greek word being *Abba*, which is a very personal

---

98   Ibid., 24.

term for father, an equivalent in English being "Daddy."[99] So Jesus modeled for his disciples the importance of spending time alone and in prayer, in which the relationship with God was very close. Jesus tells us, "Believe me that I am in the Father and Father is in me."[100] He is conscious of the Indwelling Divine Presence.

How Should We Pray?

When Jesus taught His disciples, he specifically told them:

> When you pray, go to your inner room, close the door, and pray to your Father in secret. And your Father who sees in secret will repay you.[101]

In ancient times, the Desert Fathers and Mothers interpreted the "inner room" as the silent recesses of the heart where the human and Divine meet. St. Paul adds:

> The Spirit comes to the aid of our weakness; for we do not know how to pray as we ought, but the Spirit itself intercedes with inexpressible groanings. And the one who searches hearts knows the intention of the Spirit, because it intercedes for the holy ones according to God's will.[102]

"Prayer is the lofty gift of God to man."[103] It can be simply described as the workings of the Holy Spirit within us. Our desire is to get in touch with these workings of the Spirit, our intention is direct contact

---

99   See Albert Nolan, *Jesus Before Christianity* (Maryknoll, NY: Orbis Books, 2013) 97. "*Abba* does not simply mean father. It is the very intimate, familiar form of address reserved for the intimate family circle. It might best be translated 'dad' or 'papa.'"

100 John 14:11.

101 Matt. 6:6.

102 Rom. 8:26-27.

103 A Monk of Mount Athos, *The Watchful Mind: Teachings on the Prayer of the Heart,* transl. George Dokos (Yonkers, NY: St. Vladimir's Seminary Press, 2014), 7.

with the Divine. We need to listen for the Spirit working within us and, to do this, requires stillness and silence in our hearts. Yet, when we take time to sit in silence, to be with the Lord, one likely experiences constant distraction, the continuous bombardment of thoughts—"inner chaos going on in our heads, like some wild cocktail party of which we find ourselves the embarrassed host."[104] We seek interior silence and discover inner noise instead. Our challenge is to listen for the voice of Jesus, to experience the Divine Presence, within the silent recesses of our hearts. The Jesus Prayer is a powerful tool to help us achieve inner stillness.

An Ancient Prayer Tradition Focusing on Interior Stillness

While the Jesus Prayer is not the only form of contemplative prayer, it is one of the most ancient forms, the origin of which can be traced back to the Desert Fathers and Mothers. While historically not as well known in the Roman Church and the Christian West, the Jesus Prayer has always been an important component of the spirituality of Eastern Christians, Catholic and Orthodox. Its practice even today remains widespread in the Christian East. Given the flourishing monastic communities in Eastern Europe, Ukraine, and Russia, and the large Coptic communities in Egypt, the Jesus Prayer is likely the most widely-used form of contemplative prayer. In more recent times, a number of Western Christian spiritual writers are increasingly referencing this method of prayer, especially given the increasing awareness of the importance of contemplation as a means for an encounter with the Lord Jesus.[105] The beauty of the Jesus Prayer is its absolute simplicity.

---

104 Martin Laird, *Into the Silent Land: A Guide to the Christian Practice of Contemplation* (Oxford University Press, 2006), 4.

105 As examples, Dorothy Day wrote an article entitled, "The Prayer of Jesus," *The Catholic Worker Movement,* Third Hour #6 (1954), 13-18. She wrote this article after reading the Russian classic, *The Way of a Pilgrim.* See http://www.catholicworker.org/dorothyday/ Reprint2.cfm?TextID=883. A co-worker of Day's, Jim Forest, wrote, *The Road to Emmaus: Pilgrimage as a Way of Life* (Maryknoll, NY: Orbis Books, 2007). This book makes frequent references to Chariton of Valamo's *The Art of Prayer: An Orthodox Anthology,* which is considered an Eastern Christian spiritual classic.

Brief Historical Overview

The following provides a brief overview of the historical development of the Jesus Prayer and how it has been faithfully practiced and preserved from ancient times to the present.

1. Prayer instituted by Jesus (Invocation of the Name)

Some spiritual writers believe the Jesus Prayer is a divine institution, not instituted through a prophet, not by the words of apostle, not through the mediation of an angel, but established by the Son of God and God himself.[106] At the conclusion of the Last Supper, Jesus established the prayer in his name:

> Amen, amen, I say to you, whatever you ask the Father in my name he will give you. Until now you have not asked anything in my name; ask and you will receive, so that your joy may be complete.[107]

Previously, the disciples had some experience with the name of Jesus. For example, when the 72 disciples returned from their mission, they rejoiced, saying, "Lord, even the demons are subject to us because of your name."[108] They healed and cured in the name of Jesus, so they already understood, at least to a limited extent, there was power in the name of Jesus. As he told them, "Whatever you ask in my name, I will do, so that the Father may be glorified in the Son. If you ask anything of me in my name, I will do it."[109] Post-Ascension, we see evidence of this invocation in the Acts of Apostles. When Peter cured the crippled beggar,

---

106 See Brianchaninov, *The Refuge*, 195.
107 John 16:23-24.
108 Luke 10:17.
109 John 14:13-14.

he said, "I have neither silver nor gold, but what I do have I give you: in the name of Jesus Christ the Nazorean, rise and walk."[110] When the apostles were taken into custody and Peter gave testimony before the Sanhedrin, he said, "There is no salvation through anyone else, nor is there any other name under heaven given to the human race by which we are to be saved."[111] Accordingly, some spiritual writers point to the invocation of the name of Jesus evidenced in the Acts of the Apostles.[112] As Brianchaninov wrote, "The Jesus Prayer was universally practiced by the Christians of the first centuries ..."[113]

2. The Desert Fathers and Mothers (third to fifth century Egypt)

In the Third through Fifth Centuries, the Desert Fathers and Mothers withdrew into the Egyptian and later the Syrian deserts for solitude in imitation of Jesus. They developed a unique form of contemplative prayer known as *hesychia* (ἡσυχία), which in Greek means stillness, watchfulness, and interior silence of the heart. This came to be known as the hesychast prayer tradition,[114] which is also sometimes referred to as Prayer of the Heart or, simply by many monks, as just "the Prayer." It continued to grow and be refined, creating what ultimately became known as the Jesus Prayer. Abba Arsenius (c. 350-445), one of the monks to withdraw to the desert, said he heard a voice telling him, "Flee, keep silent, and be at rest."[115] These three instructions are more or less the core of hesychast spirituality.[116] The Desert Fathers and

---

110 Acts 3:6.
111 Acts 4:12.
112 See Brianchaninov, *The Refuge*, 195.
113 Ibid., 209.
114 In descriptions of Catholic spirituality, the hesychast tradition is also referred to as Desert Spirituality.
115 *The Sayings of the Desert Fathers*, transl. by Benedicta Ward, SLG (Kalamazoo, MI: Cistercian Publications, 1975), xxi.
116 See George Maloney, SJ, *Prayer of the Heart: The Contemplative Tradition of the Christian East* (Notre Dame, IN: Ave Maria Press, 1981), 43.

Mothers knew that Christianity was a divinizing process that took place gradually within the human heart, the interior focus where man and the triune God meet. By constant vigilance, purification, and humility, this divinizing process would continue such that humanity could ultimately become partakers of God's divine nature.[117] Silence and solitude were to highlight an inward movement toward a more spiritual listening to God's indwelling presence.

Interior stillness is the key to prayer—the ability to move past the constant chaos in our minds, which create distractions. Thoughts and feelings encroach upon our silence. These can include anger, despair, impatience, bitterness, jealousy, sloth, past memories and hurts, concerns about the future, deadlines, anxiety, fear, or worries. Further, sometimes the distractions can seem positive (a great idea for work, homily, catechism class), and there is a temptation to believe these are of divine origin. But no matter how positive or negative the thoughts, these are all distractions. The absence of this chaos of thoughts equates to interior stillness, and that is what we want in order to encounter the Living Jesus, the Divine Presence dwelling within us.

The hesychast prayer tradition evolved as a means to achieve this inner stillness. As Abba Macarius (300-91) advised when asked by one of the brothers how one should pray:

> There is no need for long discourses. It is enough to stretch out one's hands and to say, 'Lord, as you will, and as you know, have mercy.' And if the conflict grows fiercer, say: 'Lord, help!' He knows very well what we need and he shows us his mercy.[118]

---

117 See 2 Pt. 1:4.
118 *Sayings of the Desert Fathers*, 131.

Short, simple orations were used to fix the mind on the presence of God. From the Gospels, the cry of the blind man on the road to Jericho was, "Lord, Jesus Christ, son of David, have pity on me."[119] The humble prayer of the publican (tax collector) was, "O God, be merciful to me a sinner."[120] These became the prayers of the Desert Fathers and Mothers, along with the litany of the liturgy, *Kyrie eleison* ("Lord, have mercy"). St. John Cassian (360-435), who spent time with the monks in the desert before heading to the West, described in his *Conferences* his particular prayer: "Come to my help, O God; Lord, hurry to my rescue."[121] In the Ethiopian tradition, the prayer was: "Jesus, have mercy on me! Jesus, help me! I praise you, my God!"[122] This desert prayer tradition remained strong with the monastics in Egypt, Palestine, and Syria into the ninth century and is the origin of the Jesus Prayer.

3. Greek Monastic Revival (beginning in the thirteenth century)

In the thirteenth and fourteenth centuries, there was a renaissance of the hesychast prayer tradition in the East, particularly in the monasteries on Mount Athos in Greece, which even today is the center of Orthodox monastic spirituality. Nikodemos of the Holy Mountain (1749-1809) and Makarios of Corinth (1731-1805) "published the *Philokalia*, a collection of the writings and sayings of 24 great ascetic Fathers of the church,"[123] spanning the fourth to fifteenth centuries.[124] These writings include those of St. Symeon the New Theologian (949-1022), Nicephoros (ca 1300), St. Gregory of Sinai (ca

---

119 Luke 18:38.
120 Luke 18:13.
121 Psalm 69:2.
122 See Bunge, *Earthen Vessels*, 120.
123 George S. Bebis, "Nikodimos of the Holy Mountain," *Encyclopedia of Religion*, ed. Lindsay Jones, 2nd ed., vol. 10, (Detroit: Macmillan Reference USA, 2005, 6621). *Gale Virtual Reference Library*. Web. 27 Sept. 2014.
124 Philip Sheldrake, *Spirituality: A Brief History*, 2nd ed. (Singapore: Wiley-Blackwell, 2013), 156.

1265 – 1346), and others, culminating in the great defense of the hesychast tradition by St. Gregory Palamas (1296-1359). It was at this time the "formula" of the Jesus Prayer as we know it today ("Lord, Jesus Christ, Son of God, have mercy on me, a sinner") and the techniques of how to synchronize this prayer with one's breathing, the sitting position, and so forth, began to be specified.

The hesychast tradition expanded to such places as Romania, Ukraine, and Russia. A number of well-known Russian mystics associated with this tradition, such as Nil Sorsky (d. 1508),[125] began to emerge.

4. Russian Spiritual Renaissance (eighteenth century)

In the eighteenth century, Russia underwent a spiritual renaissance attributed to Paisius Velichkovsky (1722-94). He was a monk who spent time at the monasteries on Mount Athos and then became an elder at the Optina hermitage,[126] which became a significant spiritual center in Russia. Velichkovsky was familiar with the Jesus Prayer and coordinated the translation of various spiritual books from Greek and Latin into Russian, including the *Philokalia*.[127] Two elements of this spiritual renaissance are worth mentioning. First was the appearance of the *starchestvo*.[128] The *staretz* (literally, "old man") was a spiritual father (sometimes called an elder) and a guide of souls who, even though not always a priest, attracted people to himself because of his experience in the spiritual life, his special gifts, and, above all, his discernment of spirits.[129] Three well-known examples of such elders are St. Seraphim of Sarov,

---

125 Also known as Nilus of Sora.
126 "Monasticism: VI. Eastern Monasticism Since 1453," *New Catholic Encyclopedia Supplement 2010*, ed. Robert L. Fastiggi, Vol. 2, (Detroit: Gale, 2010) 817-821. *Gale Virtual Reference Library*. Web. 24 Sept. 2014. 821.
127 Ibid.
128 Defined as a lineage of spiritual wisdom of prayer maintained by a *staretz*, or spiritual elder.
129 "Monasticism: VI. Eastern Monasticism Since 1453," 821.

St. Ignatius Brianchaninov, and St. Theophan the Recluse. The second element is that the rich prayer tradition of the monks on Mount Athos was brought to the lay people in Russia, Ukraine, and Romania. People from all walks of life, peasant to royalty, would come to the monasteries in Russia to seek the spiritual counsels of the elders (spiritual direction). It was also during this renaissance that the spiritual classic, The Pilgrim's Tale,[130] was published with the oldest redaction coming from the Optina Monastery. In this classic, the unknown pilgrim, who is portrayed as a simple peasant, is advised in the progress of his spiritual life by an elder, who uses the Jesus Prayer as a starting point for spiritual discipline.

Another well-known name in the Russian tradition is St. John of Kronstadt (1829-1908). Living in extreme poverty, he was known as a man of prayer[131] and developed a compassionate love for neighbor. Continuing in the tradition of the staretz, John was unique because he was a parish priest, not a monk. Yet his counsel was sought by all societal classes across Russia, nobility and peasant alike. He is considered a major influence on lay Christians. His spirituality had three important tenets: (1) daily Eucharist is central; (2) charity is inherent to Christian piety; and (3) the importance of personal prayer.[132] "His spiritual diary, My Life in Christ, is a classic of contemporary Russian Orthodox spirituality."[133]

5. The Hesychast Prayer Tradition Today

Today, the Jesus Prayer is the most widely used form of contemplative prayer in the world. Its origins can be clearly

---

130 The Pilgrim's Tale, transl. by T. Allan Smith, "Introduction" by Aleksei Pentkovsky, taken from The Classics of Western Spirituality series (Mahwah, NJ: Paulist Press, 1999). In other translations, this work is also known as The Way of the Pilgrim.

131 Thomas Hopko, "Ioann of Kronstadt," Encyclopedia of Religion, ed. Lindsay Jones. 2nd ed., Vol. 7 (Detroit: Macmillan Reference USA, 2005) 4532. Gale Virtual Reference Library, Web, 26 Nov. 2014.

132 Sheldrake, Spirituality: A Brief History, 196.

133 Hopko, "Ioann of Kronstadt."

traced to the experiences and writings of the Desert Fathers and Mothers—their withdrawal, detachment, asceticism, focus on silent contemplation, and carrying forth their relationship with God through love of neighbor. Interest in the Jesus Prayer has been increasing in the United States and the Christian West. One notable example of a spiritual father from the hesychast tradition and someone who was counter-cultural was Elder Ephraim of Arizona. A disciple of a renown spiritual elder from Mount Athos (Elder Joseph the Hesychast, 1897-1959), Ephraim became the abbot of Philotheou Monastery, which he reformed into the hesychast tradition.[134] In 1979, he came to North America for medical treatment and began to discuss the spiritual well-being of Orthodox Christians with various bishops and parishes. He found that many were using ethnic festivals and treating people with drinks, food, and entertainment. For many, the churches had taken on a social dimension, arguably responding to the spirit of the age. As one priest described it:

> And then a tiny man came, without worldly education and theological diplomas, without innovative and bold ideas (which we had in abundance) and reminded us of the most important thing—our Tradition! He did not call for dancing and entertainment, but called for fasting and participation in hours-long vigils. And people *responded* to his call, came to the old man and supported him![135]

Elder Ephraim established 17 monasteries in the U.S. and Canada, in stark contrast to the culture of consumption and

---

134 The disciples of Elder Joseph reformed numerous monasteries on Mount Athos, creating a resurgence in the Jesus Prayer tradition.

135 Written by Fr. Anthony Moschonas, originally from Tucson, Arizona. Post by Alexander Poshtaruk to the *Face Book* page, "Ask About the Orthodox Faith," December 10, 2019. Elder Ephraim had reposed in the Lord on December 7, 2019.

slavery to material goods. People were led to rediscover their undistorted Christian values. As Elder Porphyrios said, "We mustn't compromise the magnificence of our faith."[136] How true!

It is worth noting that in the Roman Church's Rite of Penance, the tenth form of the Act of Contrition (and the shortest) is, "Lord Jesus, Son of God, have mercy on me, a sinner,"[137] which is essentially the Jesus Prayer.

Prayer is the Path to God

The primary purpose of the Jesus Prayer is to assist us to deepen our relationship with Jesus Christ by encountering him in the stillness of the human heart. It is like the example of Martha grousing, overwhelmed with the chores of hospitality, while her sister Mary sat listening at the feet of Jesus. He told her that Mary had chosen "the better portion."[138] This form of prayer, like listening at the feet of Jesus, can help us set aside all earthly cares,[139] allowing our hearts to be lifted up to God. Prayer is the path to God, for whom every human heart longs either consciously or unconsciously.

---

136 Elder Porphyrios, *Wounded by Love*, 211.
137 *Rite of Penance* (Totowa, NJ: Catholic Book Publishing Corp, 2009), 39. Act of Contrition, Form No. 10.
138 See Luke 10:38-42. For a discussion of the Mary-Martha dynamic, see Deacon and Pilgrim, *Hearts Afire: Fulfilling Our Destiny* (Fairfax, VA: Eastern Christian Publications, 2014), 49-54. Conference No. 7. "First Things First."
139 Consider the words of the Cherubic Hymn in the Divine Liturgy of St. John Chrysostom.

Rising very early before dawn,
he left and went off to a
deserted place, where he prayed.

(Mark 1:35)

CHAPTER 3

Encountering the Risen Jesus

"I have neither silver nor gold, but what I do have I give you ..."
(Acts 3:6)

"His name is living. It gives new life to those who cry out
with it to the source of Life, the Lord Jesus Christ."[140]
(St. Ignatius Brianchaninov)

"The simpler, better, and more loving a person is, the more blessed he is
inwardly; the more deceitful, evil, and selfish he is, the more unhappy."[141]
(St. John of Kronstadt)

Opening Gospel Passage

Read: Matt. 6:19-34 (Dependence on God).

Discovering the Treasure (Deposit of Faith)

If we became aware of a vast treasure, infinitely valuable, would we not want to make the effort to find it? Peter said to the cripple, "I have neither silver nor gold, but what I do have I give you ..."[142] As Jesus told his disciples through parables:

> The kingdom of heaven is like a treasure buried in a field, which a person finds and hides again, and out of joy goes and sells all that he has and buys that field. Again, the kingdom of heaven is like a merchant

---

140 Brianchaninov, *The Refuge*, 202.
141 St. John of Kronstadt, *My Life in Christ*, Part 1, transl. E. E. Goulaeff. Revised and adapted by Nicholas Kotar (Jordanville, NY: Holy Trinity Monastery, 2015), 91.
142 Acts 3:6.

searching for fine pearls. When he finds a pearl of great price, he goes and sells all that he has and buys it.[143]

Our Deposit of Faith is a valuable treasure, and contained therein is a profound mystical prayer tradition, the Jesus Prayer, which has the power to transform lives. In today's day and age, it often seems as if we have become complacent with this precious treasure and are in need of rediscovering it.

Putting the Teachings of Jesus into Context

Matthew Kelly wrote in his book, *Rediscover the Saints*:

> Nothing will change a person's life like really learning how to pray. It's one of life's most powerful lessons. And yet, astonishingly, we don't teach people how to talk to God. We don't teach them to pray with their hearts in a deeply personal way. It is one of the areas of singular importance where we have fallen short as a Church.[144]

St. John of Kronstadt wrote, "It is indispensable for every Christian to acquire the habit of turning quickly to God in prayer about everything, since we are weak, and he is the source of all power and goodness."[145] An anonymous, current-day monk of Mount Athos explained: "Combined with inner purification and a regular sacramental life, a life of prayer will help significantly in the regeneration of the faithful during this difficult period in which we live."[146]

To put this into further perspective, Mother Teresa had a very simple philosophy: "Pray and trust." It is that simple and yet that hard because to trust someone, we must personally know him or her. To

---

143 Matt. 13:44-46.
144 Matthew Kelly, *Rediscover the Saints*, 31.
145 St. John of Kronstadt, *My Life in Christ*, Part 1, 57.
146 Monk Moses of Mount Athos, *Athonite Flowers: Seven Contemporary Essays on the Spiritual Life*, transl. Fr. Peter A. Chamberas (Brookline, MA: Holy Cross Press, 2000), 60.

have a personal relationship with Jesus Christ, to come to love him and trust him above all else, we must come to know him through prayer. We must learn to truly pray.[147]

Cultivating Prayer and a Love for Jesus

When we met him, Fr. Menas al Macarius was a 91-year-old monk who spent the past 53 years as a hermit living outside the Monastery of St. Macarius in Egypt's Wadi al Natron. He only recently began accepting a few visitors at his hermitage. In the wisdom he shared with his visitors on April 1, 2019, Fr. Menas was quite empathetic: "Without prayer, without Jesus, we have nothing."[148] He advised that we should daily recite with our whole hearts, "Jesus, Jesus, I love you. Jesus, Jesus, I love you." Children, he said, are part of this; by age 10, they should learn to love Jesus. Prayer is critical to such a relationship.

The hermitage of Fr. Menas, outside of the walls of
St. Macarius Monastery, Wadi al Natron, Egypt, April 1, 2019.

147 See Evagrius Ponticus, *The Praktikos & Chapters on Prayer*, transl. John Eudes Bamberger, OCSO (Kalamazoo, MI: Cistercian Publications, 1972), 65. "If you are a theologian you truly pray. If you truly pray you are a theologian."
148 Fr. Menas al Macarius, April 1, 2019. This hermit shared his wisdom with a few visitors, including the author.

The Living Jesus is meant to be experienced. It is through our encounters with him that personal transformation occurs. The busyness of our lives often takes away from time to cultivate a genuine rule of prayer. Jesus was a busy person, too, constantly in demand, teaching people, and curing the afflicted of their ailments. Yet, he withdrew to deserted places to be alone with his Father, providing us with an example of how we need time to be refreshed and renewed, cultivating the Divine Presence within. Accordingly, we need to make time to create a relationship with God through prayer, to listen to his voice in silence and solitude.

Conditions for Prayer – Exterior and Interior Stillness

We need to create the right environment in order to gain greater awareness of living in the presence of Christ. We need to flee the noise and busyness of the world through exterior and interior silence. St. John Climacus, in his seminal work, *The Ladder of Divine Ascent*, describes this as a three-part process:[149]

First	Detachment from concern with regard to the necessary and unnecessary. This involves examining our own self-denial and withdrawal from the trappings of our lives. "The first task of stillness is disengagement from every affair, good and bad, since concern with the former leads on to the latter."[150]
Second	Urgent prayer; experiencing a genuine need for prayer in our lives.
Third	Unremitting action of prayer in the heart, or "Prayer without ceasing."

---

149 See St. John Climacus, *The Ladder of Divine Ascent*, transl. Colm Luibheid and Norman Russell (New York: Paulist Press, 1982), 268. Step 27, "On Stillness."
150 Ibid.

For the Early Desert Fathers and Mothers, the wilderness provided an environment conducive to exterior stillness, which would be conducive to interior silence. We, in turn, can learn lessons from this Desert Spirituality. While we may not be able to move to the desert, we can empty ourselves through ascetical practices, free ourselves from worldly attachments, unshackle ourselves from bitterness and anger, surrender our self-will to the Divine will—freeing ourselves from distractions—so we can similarly begin to cultivate the conditions for interior stillness. This calmness allows us to encounter God in prayer, to be filled by his presence.

The Work of Prayer

The objective of hesychast prayer is interior stillness—a freeing from thoughts and other distractions, and an openness that creates an awareness of the presence of God. In the three-phase process of St. John Climacus, he cites a continuous desire to experience God in prayer. This type of "pure prayer" is a gift from God, granted to mystics who, in turn, experience a sense of union with him. As one modern spiritual elder from Mount Athos describes it:

> When God comes into our heart, he gains victory over the devil and cleanses the impurities which the evil one has created. The victory, therefore, over the devil is the victory of Christ in us. Let us do the human part by inviting Christ, and he will do the divine part by defeating the devil and purifying us.[151]

This anonymous elder also explained that the Jesus Prayer consists of two basic points of doctrine: acknowledges the divinity of Christ

---

151 Metropolitan Hierotheos of Nafpaktos, *A Night in the Desert of the Holy Mountain: Discussion with a Hermit on the* Jesus *Prayer*, transl. Effie Mavromichali (Levadia, Greece: Birth of the Theotokos Monastery, 2009), 44. Metropolitan Hierotheos interviewed a spiritual elder who desired at the time to remain anonymous. In 2019, a monk from Holy Archangels Greek Orthodox Monastery in Kendalia, Texas informed the author that this spiritual elder, now deceased, had been a disciple of Elder Joseph the Hesychast, similar to Elder Ephraim of Arizona.

("Lord Jesus Christ, Son of God") and confesses our inability to be saved through our own merits ("Have mercy on me").[152] Jesus tells us that the Father in heaven already knows what we need before we ask.[153] Accordingly, all we truly need from God is his mercy. This acknowledges surrender of self-will to the Divine will ("Not my will but yours be done"[154]). The anonymous elder also explained: "We are not struggling to meet an impersonal God through the Jesus Prayer. We do not seek our elevation to absolute nothingness. Our prayer focuses on the personal God, the God-man Jesus."[155]

With continued practice, the individual will experience an insatiable thirst for the Jesus Prayer.[156] Yet, at the same time, virtually all Spiritual Fathers and Mothers have said that attaining true prayer is a struggle. We are under constant attacks by the demons that wish to steal our prayer and derail our relationship with God. These distractions are often referred to as *logismoi*—either positive or negative thoughts or impulses—which cause one to drift away from interior stillness and prayer.[157] Accordingly, we must remain persistent in our prayer, maintain our ardent desire, persevere in hope, retain our zeal, and exhibit immense patience—all combined with faith in the love God has for us.[158] As St. Silouan the Athonite (1866-1938) advised:

> There is no comfortable armchair in the study for the
> monk to work out these problems. In the silence of the

---

152 Ibid., 45.
153 Cf. Matt. 6:8.
154 Luke 22:42. Also Matt. 26:39 and Mark 14:36. In John 6:38, Jesus states during his Bread of Life Discourse, "[B]ecause I came down from heaven not to do my own will but the will of the one who sent me." Throughout his ministry, Jesus models and describes the importance of complete obedience to the Father, so much so that it is included in the prayer he taught his disciples: "Your will be done on earth as in heaven" (Matt. 6:10).
155 Metropolitan Hierotheos of Nafpaktos, *A Night in the Desert of the Holy Mountain*, 50.
156 Ibid. See 170–171.
157 See A Deacon and Fellow Pilgrim, *Hearts Afire: A Personal Encounter with Jesus*, 2nd ed. (Fairfax, VA: Eastern Christian Publications, 2016), 34. Reference is made to *The Pilgrim's Tale*, in which attacks from the left are vain thoughts and sinful imaginings. Attacks from the right are edifying memories or beautiful thoughts. Both of these are distractions with one intent: to disrupt one's prayer and relationship with God.
158 Ibid., 81.

night, remote from the world, unheard and unseen, he falls down before God and weeps the prayer of the publican, "God be merciful to me, a sinner," or cries with St. Peter, "Lord, save me!"[159]

Elder Porphyrios, a monk who spent time on Mount Athos, advised:

Learn to love prayer. In order not to live in darkness, turn on the switch of prayer so that divine light may flood your soul. Christ will appear in the depths of your being. There, in the deepest and most inward part, is the Kingdom of God. The Kingdom of God is within you.[160]

Prayer nurtures our personal, intimate relationship with God, who asks that of us. Contemplation is not about doing, but more about a state of being, an increased awareness of God's presence, and that our true selves are intrinsically tied to God. In the instructions of Abba Arsenius, contemplation is to be at rest (being, not doing). As St. Isaac the Syrian (640-700) wrote, "The soul that loves God rests only in God."[161]

It is worth saying again that prayer is a gift from God, who makes the first move toward us and desires to spend time with us through our prayer (entering into relationship). Our role is to make ourselves available, expressing our love for God by spending time in prayerful recollection and persevering through the struggles, which we will invariably experience because the demons always want to disrupt any time spent with God. Such opposition and struggles are actually indicative of progress, so we should never give up.

---

159 Archimandrite Sophrony Sakharov, *St. Silouan the Athonite*, transl. Rosemary Edmonds (Crestwood, NY: St. Vladimir's Seminary Press, 1991), 166.
160 Elder Porphyrios, *Wounded by Love*, 113.
161 *The Ascetical Homilies of Saint Isaac the Syrian*, rev. 2nd ed. (Boston: Holy Transfiguration Monastery, 2011), 141. Homily Four.

The Jesus Prayer

The Jesus Prayer is a simple, yet powerful tool for assisting us in achieving interior stillness and coming to know the Lord Jesus in a personal way. In effect, it places Jesus at the center of our lives. This is an overview of the most common form of the prayer itself:

Breathing[162]	Prayer[163]	Observation
Inhale	*Lord, Jesus Christ*[164]	***A profession of faith:*** Acknowledging Jesus as Lord, the center of our lives and as the Son of God.
Exhale	*Son of God*	
Inhale	*Have mercy on me*	***A desire for repentance and reconciliation:*** Acknowledging who we are ("a sinner") and our request of Jesus ("have mercy on me"). In addition, the prayer is grounded in humility—the foundation for attaining all the other virtues. Humility is part of the movement away from self, surrendering self-will to the Divine will.
Exhale	*A sinner*	

---

162 Some Spiritual Fathers would advise their disciples that the prayer is said on a single breath: (Inhale) "Lord Jesus Christ, Son of God"; (exhale) "have mercy on me, a sinner." Either means is acceptable, as long as the prayer itself becomes as natural as breathing. To some, this two-breath approach more readily adapts to a natural breathing pattern. Ultimately, it is up to the practitioner to decide what is better.

163 In the writings of the Holy Fathers, one may encounter variants of the Jesus Prayer. Some Greek Fathers use a shorter version: "Lord Jesus Christ, have mercy on me." Others may exclude the phrase "a sinner," originally added in the Russian/Slavic tradition. Each still contains the two key components of the prayer: the invocation of the name of Jesus and the request for what we most need: mercy. Herein we use the most common form and that which we were taught by our Spiritual Fathers.

164 Acts 4:12: "There is no salvation through anyone else, nor is there any other *name* under heaven given to the human race by which we are to be saved."

This prayer acknowledges a complete surrender to God, allowing Jesus to lead us on the spiritual journey to the Father. The Jesus Prayer is the only contemplative prayer tradition that approaches God with such a profound sense of humility. In today's world, there seems to be a loss of respect for God. This prayer focuses on the right-ordered relationship between Creator and creature, acknowledging the great difference between them and asking for the one thing we most need: *mercy*. We need not ask for anything more because Jesus tells us: "Your Father knows what you need before you ask him."[165] As one contemporary Athonite monk described it, this is a prayer of the fallen person who acknowledges his or her sinfulness and, through the invocation of this prayer, asks God for divine mercy and light. "It is the language God loves to hear."[166] Consider the return of the prodigal son, acknowledging, "Father, I have sinned …"[167]

It is important to note the Jesus Prayer is performed without mental forms or focusing on images, such as an icon. It does not involve imagination or any form of thoughts. Rather, it is solely intended as a means to experience the presence of God. The breathing is meant to be natural, such that the prayer takes root in the heart, even when the practitioner is not conscious of it ("praying without ceasing"[168]).

Practicing the Jesus Prayer

Some practical thoughts on saying the Jesus Prayer[169]:

1. **Posture** – Position your body comfortably, spine erect, using either a chair or cushions. Athonite elders recommend a low stool, closer to the ground as a posture of humility. Bow the head as we come humbly before our Creator. Recall the

---

165 Matt. 6:8.
166 Monk Moses, *Athonite Flowers*, 41.
167 Luke 15:21.
168 Cf. 1 Thess. 5:17.
169 The framework below leverages material from the following source: Ken Kaisch, *Finding God: A Handbook of Christian Meditation* (New York: Paulist Press, 1994), 199-200.

Publican (tax collector) who "would not even raise his eyes to heaven."[170]

2. **Be Grounded** – Be aware of your physical senses. Close your eyes and gradually become aware of the physical senses of your body. Feel them as they flow through you.

3. **Open Your Awareness to God's Presence** – Feel the presence of God all around. Feel that presence within. Breathe in the Divine with every breath. Breathe God out, and let yourself rest in his presence. Begin slow, steady breathing with deep, natural breaths—not prolonged, but natural. Release outside thoughts and distractions.

4. **Move Thoughts from the Head to the Heart** – With every breath, allow the sphere of energy within to slowly sink from the head to the heart. This may be very difficult at first; slowly allow the energy within to become heavier and heavier, sinking to the heart one inch at a time. Center yourself in your heart. This is why the Jesus Prayer is also referred to as "Prayer of the Heart." St. Ignatius Brianchaninov wrote:

   > The attentiveness of the mind during prayer attracts the heart in sympathy. When attentiveness becomes natural to prayer, then the mind can descend into the heart for most profound prayerful worship.[171]

5. **Begin the Words of the Prayer** – When a rhythm of breathing has been established, synchronize your breathing with the reverent repetition of the prayer. Slowly say the words from the heart: "*Lord, Jesus Christ, Son of God, have mercy on me, a sinner.*" Let your heart repeat these words slowly, over and

---

170 Luke 18:13.
171 Brianchaninov, *The Refuge*, 219.

over again, feeling God's presence within. St. John Climacus writes: "The beginning of prayer is the expulsion of distractions from the very start by a single thought."[172] In this case, that single thought is the Jesus Prayer.

6. **Be Attentive** – When your attention wanders, be patient. Thoughts and distractions are likely to emerge in one's consciousness during the Jesus Prayer (we can experience interior chaos in our minds, a constant bombardment of thoughts). Slowly refocus on the prayer, releasing the thoughts. "The goal is not to suppress the thoughts during prayer, but only to ignore them, to let them be and to let them go—and to *prefer* Jesus, to choose him anew whenever we wander."[173]

Fr. Thomas Keating, OCSO (1923-2018), provided the best analogy for thoughts. He described human consciousness as a river and our thoughts as boats going down the river.[174] Suddenly in prayer, we realize that we are on one of these boats. Keating wrote: "If you find yourself on a boat, just get off. There should be no self-recriminations, no sighs, no annoyance that you had a thought. Any such reflection is another thought, another boat."[175]

We should not judge ourselves for having a thought. Just gently let it go and return to the prayer. Remember the intention: to enter into prayer, to cultivate the relationship with God. God is more interested in our intention than whether we do the prayer perfectly, which we cannot. Gently we bring ourselves back to attentiveness (head in the heart, rhythmically breathing, and the slow repetition of the prayer: *Lord, Jesus Christ, Son of God, have mercy on me, a sinner*).

---

172 St. John Climacus, *The Ladder of Divine Ascent*, 276. Step 28: "On Prayer." The Greek term used for thought, *monologistōs*, can also mean "by a repeated short prayer."
173 Joseph Langford, MC, *Mother Teresa's Secret Fire*, 196.
174 See Thomas Keating, *Intimacy with God* (New York: The Crossroad Publishing Company, 2002), 61-63.
175 Ibid., 63.

Consider the Four "R's" related to interior stillness:

- Do not **Resist** the thought. We are human beings; rational thought is part of who we are. It was a gift from our Creator.

- Do not **Retain** the thought. Once you realize your mind has wandered, gently release the thought. If you find yourself on a boat, simply get off.

- Gently **Return** to the prayer. Reestablish the rhythm and pattern.

- Do not **Regret** the thought. The purpose of the prayer is intention—to build a relationship with the unseen God, who knows this intention. Regret is another thought, another boat going down the river. Regret is also a demon that can result in despair and discouragement, preventing us from continuing our prayer or simply giving up.

The repetition of the prayer is not a monotonous attempt to gain God's attention,[176] essentially trying to wear God down, but an attempt to change oneself by clearing one's mind of everything except Jesus. The goal is to make this prayer so connected with one's breathing that it becomes, as the experienced Spiritual Fathers say, truly rooted in our hearts and continues as unconscious or self-activating prayer.

Regarding distractions (*logismoi*), the "enemy" who despises prayer will do *anything* to disrupt our efforts. Assaults come from the left ("vain thoughts and sinful imaginings"[177]) and from the right ("edifying memories" or "beautiful thoughts"[178]). All such thoughts are meant to disrupt us from

---

176 Cf. Matt. 6:7.
177 *The Pilgrim's Tale*, 108.
178 Ibid.

our prayer. Keep in mind what is important to God. He is pleased when we persevere in our prayer; we stay the course, no matter how intense the distractions become.

Finally, here is the reality. Our practice is not "never let your attention in prayer be stolen." It will most definitely be stolen, perhaps every three seconds or every 30 seconds. Our practice is to cultivate the habit of returning to the prayer, to return to the present, which in turn cultivates stillness.[179]

7. **Conclude the Jesus Prayer** – When you are ready, let the feeling return to your hands, feet, and face. Take a deep breath and slowly open your eyes. This prayer was intended for a monastic to perform in his or her cell. Accordingly, each person chooses when to conclude his or her prayer. The prayer is not about completing a specified number of repetitions. What is most important is to simply spend quality — not quantity — time in silence with Jesus.

8. **Use a Prayer Rope** – Eastern Catholic monastics often use a prayer rope to count the number of recitations of the Jesus Prayer. It also helps one remain focused on the prayer. Tradition has it that St. Pachomius (292-348), an Egyptian and early Desert Father, invented the prayer rope as an aid for illiterate monks to accomplish a consistent number of prayers and prostrations in their cells.

179 Laird, *Into the Silent Land*, 43.

Prayer ropes come in varying lengths; however, ropes with 100 beads (usually with a knotted cross on the end) and 33 beads are the most common.

The Jesus Prayer is meant to be personal, done in private to reflect the instructions of Jesus in Matt. 6:6 ("Enter the inner room, close the door, and pray to your Father in secret"). St. Isaac the Syrian tells us we cannot taste honey by reading a book.[180] God is not meant to be intellectualized; he is meant to be experienced. Similarly, we can continue to discuss the history and merits of the Jesus Prayer; however, it is more important for us to experience the prayer, to taste its sweetness, and be sustained by its fruits. Take time to pause, to be still, and to enter into the Jesus Prayer.

Correlation between Prayer and Service

There is a direct correlation between a personal encounter with Jesus and action, often in the form of service. Recall Mother Teresa's Simple Path:

The fruit of silence is prayer.
The fruit of prayer is faith.
The fruit of faith is love.
The fruit of love is service ...

Prayer cultivates the relationship with Jesus, nurturing our faith and trust in him. Based on the experience of Jesus, we are motivated to share him with others. Recall the two disciples who were en route to Emmaus. As Pope St. John Paul II wrote, "Those who have had genuine contact with Christ cannot keep him for themselves;

---

180 See *The Ascetical Homilies of Saint Isaac the Syrian*, 153. Homily Four. "Therefore, O man, pay attention to what you read here. Indeed, can these things be known from [*writings of*] ink? Or can the taste of honey pass over the palate by reading books? For if you do not strive, you will not find, and if you do not knock at the door with vehemence and keep constant vigil before it, you will not be heard."

they must proclaim him."[181] Mother Teresa, a well-known modern contemplative, illustrated the correlation between prayer and service. Many people asked Mother Teresa what her secret was. How did she keep going despite an exhausting schedule and her poor health? Her answer was: "My secret is simple … *I pray.*"[182]

She wrote: "To love as God loves, meeting daily with him in prayer is essential. Without it love dies."[183] For her, the foundation is prayer. Mother Teresa also emphasized the importance of silence, saying, "To enter into prayer, silence is necessary, for 'in the silence of the heart God speaks.'"[184]

A priest who knew her wrote:

> Mother Teresa was convinced that prayer was something simple, easily accessible, and life-giving, and it transforms us, as no amount of effort at self-improvement ever could. In her experience, the only requirement for succeeding in prayer was to take the time, to take *more* time, to actually pray.[185]

Her advice was this: "If you want to pray better, you must pray more."[186] It should be noted that prayer is an essential element within the Constitutions of the Missionaries of Charity. It is, as Mother Teresa believed, necessary for the sisters to perform their work. She often described her order as "contemplatives in the modern world."[187]

Mother Teresa is but one example who bore witness to the fact

---

181 Pope St. John Paul II, *Novo Millennio Ineunte*, no. 40.
182 Cf. Langford, *Mother Teresa's Secret* Fire, 175.
183 Mother Teresa, *Where There is Love, There is God*, ed. Brian Kolodiejchuk, MC, PhD (New York: Image Books, 2010), 2.
184 Ibid.
185 Langford, *Mother Teresa's Secret* Fire, 188.
186 Mother Teresa. Letter to the MC Sisters, October 11, 1968. Taken from Langford, *Mother Teresa's Secret* Fire, 188.
187 Mother Teresa, Instructions to the MC Sisters, November 20, 1979. Taken from Langford, *Mother Teresa's Secret Fire*, 186.

that a heart in communion with Jesus is enkindled with a fire of love that cannot help but be shared.

As Pope Francis writes:

> Without prolonged moments of adoration, of prayerful encounter with the Word, of sincere conversation with the Lord, our work easily becomes meaningless; we lose energy as a result of our weariness and difficulties, and our fervor dies out.[188]

Therefore, the true foundation for Christian service should be grounded in prayer, the seed being planted into fertile soil such that it will be truly sustainable.

In recent times, we have seen people who have placed significant emphasis on social justice almost at the expense of or even to the exclusion of having a foundation rooted in love of God. This is a true danger because if the divine foundation is divorced from service activities, which if taken to its extremes, is tantamount to secular humanism or, even worse, Pelagianism. Cardinal Sarah warns against this, writing:

> I deplore the fact that a good many bishops and priests neglect their essential mission, which is their own sanctification and the proclamation of the Gospel of Jesus, in order to get involved with sociopolitical issues like the environment, migrants, or the homeless. Taking an interest in these debates shows praiseworthy commitment. But if they neglect evangelization and their own sanctification, their advocacy is in vain.[189]

---

188 Pope Francis, *Evangelii Gaudium*, no. 262.
189 Ibid.

This is similar to the story of Martha and Mary, in which Mary had chosen "the better portion"—listening at the feet of Jesus. It is not to dismiss the need for hospitality, which Martha lamented, but rather to note that there is a proper order to things: first things first.

Practicum

The best way to experience the power of the Jesus Prayer is by entering into it. Start practicing it and making it a part of your life. Remember, it is by encountering Jesus that our hearts and lives are filled with joy, and if we cultivate the relationship with Christ dwelling in our hearts, accepting his offer of salvation, we will be set free from sin, sorrow, inner emptiness and loneliness. Contemplative prayer is a way by which we can encounter the Divine Presence and helps round out our spiritual lives.

Do not say that it is possible to be made whole without him.
Do not say that one can possess him without knowing it.
Do not say that God does not manifest himself to man.
Do not say that man cannot perceive the divine light, or that
    it is impossible in this age!
Never is it found to be impossible, my friends.
On the contrary, it is entirely possible when one desires it.[190]

—St. Symeon the New Theologian

---

190 George A. Maloney, *St. Symeon the New Theologian: The Mystic of Fire & Light and Hymns of Divine Love* (IJA Publications, 2011), 125-132. Hymn 27.

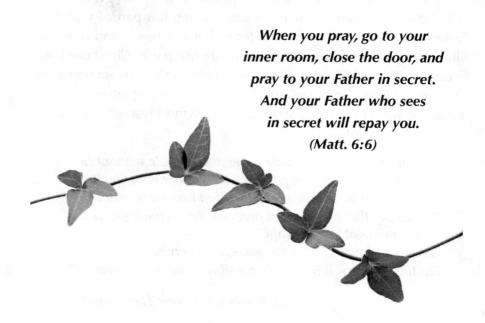

*When you pray, go to your
inner room, close the door, and
pray to your Father in secret.
And your Father who sees
in secret will repay you.
(Matt. 6:6)*

CHAPTER 4

From Encounter to Relationship

*"Pray persistently about everything, and then you will
never do anything without God's help."*[191]
(St. Mark the Ascetic)

"If you pray, you are saved. If you do not pray, you are lost."
(St. Alphonsus Liguori)

*"The soul that is in love with Christ is always joyful and happy,
however much pain and suffering this may cost ..."*[192]
(Elder Porphyrios of Kavsokalyvia)

Opening Gospel Passage

Read: Luke 18:1-8 (The Parable of the Persistent Widow).

Practical Considerations for the Jesus Prayer

As with any new skill, the Jesus Prayer takes time, practice,
persistence, and patience. In other words, there is a reason prayer
is often referred to as a "discipline," and experienced practitioners
described it as "the work of prayer." Those embarking on the journey
of cultivating a Rule of Prayer might want to consider these questions
and follow their answers as they seek a deeper relationship with the
Divine Presence:

---

191 St. Mark the Ascetic, "On Those Who Think That They are Made Righteous by Works:
Two Hundred and Twenty-Six Texts," *The Philokalia: The Complete Text*, vol. 1, comp.
St. Nikodimos of the Holy Mountain and St. Makarios of Corinth, transl. and ed. G.E.H.
Palmer, Philip Sherrard, and Kallistos Ware (New York: Faber and Faber, 1983), 133.
192 Elder Porphyrios, *Wounded by Love*, 106.

1. Why is prayer an important part of our spiritual journey?

Prayer unites our hearts to God. It is an important weapon in our inner warfare to conquer our passions and cultivate the God-like virtues on the spiritual journey to eternal blessedness. The more one "becomes adept at prayer, the closer he comes to God."[193]

Prayer is available to all. St. Seraphim of Sarov wrote:

> Among the works done for the love of Christ, prayer is the one that most readily obtains the grace of the Holy Spirit, because it is always at hand. It may happen that you want to go to church but there isn't one nearby; or else you want to help a poor man but you haven't anything to give or you do not come across one; or yet again you may want to remain chaste but natural weakness prevents you from resisting temptation. But prayer is within reach of all men and they can all give themselves to it, rich and poor, learned and unlearned, strong and weak, the sick and the healthy, the sinner and the righteous. Its power is immense; prayer more than anything else, brings us the grace of the Holy Spirit.[194]

The fullness of the interior spiritual life consists of two components: (1) the personal relationship with Jesus through prayer, and (2) the sacramental life of the Church. Both are essential and must remain in balance. This creates our love for God, which is ultimately manifested in our love for neighbor.

---

193 St. Ignatius Brianchaninov, *The Field: Cultivating Salvation*, transl. Nicholas Kotar (Jordanville, NY: Holy Trinity Publications/The Printshop of St. Job of Pochaev, 2016), 138.
194 Zander, *St. Seraphim of Sarov*, 86.

As St. Ignatius Brianchaninov would advise, "The necessary, essential condition for progress in the Jesus Prayer is living according to the commandments of the Lord Jesus. 'Abide in my Love.'"[195]

2. How does the work of prayer begin? (Repentance.)

As with any skill, the beginner must prepare the foundation (*praxis*), which means learning the associated skills. The first step is repentance. After his temptation by the devil, Jesus began his ministry by preaching and saying, "Repent, for the kingdom of heaven is at hand."[196] So, if our ultimate objective is eternal blessedness with God, until we enter the kingdom of heaven, we should "knock at its doors through repentance and prayer."[197] We should repent of all sins we have in our heart, acknowledging the teaching of Jesus: "Blessed are the clean of heart, for they shall see God."[198] Consider our hearts as vessels that have been created to receive the graces of God. They need to be as purified as possible in order to be worthy of the gift.[199] St. Ignatius Brianchaninov stated, "Nothing prepares a person for successful prayer as much as a clean conscience satisfied with God-pleasing work."[200]

Brianchaninov further advised, "The fundamental condition of successful prayer is forgiveness of all offenses, even the most grievous, without exception."[201] He is referring to the instructions of Jesus, who said, "When you stand to pray, forgive anyone against whom you have a grievance,

---

195 Brianchaninov, *The Refuge*, 256. Scripture reference is to John 15:9, which in the NABRE 2011 is translated, "Remain in my love." We need to carefully consider the teachings and examples of Jesus.
196 Matt. 4:17.
197 Brianchaninov, *The Refuge*, 134.
198 Matt. 5:8.
199 Consider also Matt. 23:26, where Jesus tells the Pharisees to "cleanse first the inside of the cup."
200 Brianchaninov, *The Field*, 142.
201 Ibid., 141.

so that your heavenly Father may in turn forgive you your transgressions."[202] Drawing from an analogy of St. Isaac the Syrian, Brianchaninov noted, "The prayer of those who recall evils done to them are seeds sown among stones."[203] As in the Parable of the Sower, such seed will not bear fruit.[204]

Repentance in the Eastern Christian spiritual tradition is not just Confession. Rather, it is a constant state of mind, being sorrowful for one's sins, mourning our sinful nature. This is also referred to as *penthos* or compunction. St. Paisios of Mount Athos (1924-94) said, "True repentance begins when a person becomes aware of his fault, is pained by it, asks forgiveness from God, and then makes his confession."[205] This ongoing state of repentance is intended for the purification of heart, making it a suitable dwelling for the Divine Presence. Thus, repentance is essential preparation in order for our prayer to bear fruit. As written in Psalm 51, "A contrite, humbled heart, O God, you will not scorn."[206] St. Ignatius Brianchaninov tells us, "Without this proper mind-set and state of heart, access to God is impossible, and all attempts and efforts are futile."[207]

3. What is the purpose of the Jesus Prayer?

The sole purpose of the Jesus Prayer is for a personal encounter with Jesus Christ, becoming aware of the Indwelling Divine Presence ("The kingdom of God is within you"[208]), and cultivating a personal relationship with him. It is not to

---

202 Mark 11:25.
203 Brianchaninov, *The Field*, 141.
204 See Matthew 13:1-13, Mark 4:1-20, and Luke 8:4-15. Reference is to the seed sown on rocky ground.
205 St. Paisios of Mount Athos, *Spiritual Struggles*. Taken from "Spiritual Counsels," vol. III, transl. by Peter Chamberas, ed. Anna Famellos and Andrinikos Masters (Souroti, Thessaloniki, Greece: Holy Monastery of Evangelist John the Theologian, 2014), 125.
206 Psalm 51:19.
207 Brianchaninov, *The Field*, 149.
208 Luke 17:21. (Orthodox Study Bible.) Patristic understanding for the translation of *entos hymōn* is "within."

gain anything, such as a prayer of petition or intercession for someone. Any benefits received are through the graces of God given to us as gift. Furthermore, Jesus told us the Father already knows what we need before we ask.[209] St. Isaac the Syrian tells us: "The highest form of prayer is to stand silently in awe before God." Accordingly, through prayer, we make ourselves available to God in a spirit of humility and spiritual poverty, desiring to enter into relationship with him.

The Jesus Prayer does not replace discursive prayer. The Jesus Prayer is an important practice to listen and enter into communion with God. However, we will continue to have other prayer practices in our lives such as the Divine Liturgy (Mass), Liturgy of the Hours (monastics are particularly fond of psalmody), other prayer practices such as the rosary, Chaplet of Divine Mercy, specific novenas, canons, akathists, and intercessory prayers for the needs of others.

4. What is the best way to start the Jesus Prayer?

Each person will create his or her own personal prayer discipline, a Rule of Prayer, such as finding a place and time to engage in the Jesus Prayer. Here are some suggestions:

a. Find a place that is conducive to your prayer practice and desire to encounter the Divine Presence. While God does not need a sacred space (all space is sacred to him), we often need our sacred place for quiet and with an appropriate atmosphere. In Eastern Christian households there is often an icon corner that generally includes an icon of Christ, an icon of the *Theotokos* (Mary, with the title bestowed upon her by the Council of Ephesus in 431, the "God-bearer," often rendered in English as "Mother of God"), and perhaps icons

---

209 Cf. Matt. 6:8.

of specific saints that have meaning to the particular household. A hand cross is also often included.

b. Stand before an icon of Christ, perhaps with a solitary candle lit before the icon, and recite the Trisagion and related prayers for one of the designated offices from the Divine Office (e.g., Third Hour[210]), really no more than a short period as a warm-up to get one's mind into the mode of prayer, especially at a very early hour. Afterward, settle into silence and begin the Jesus Prayer. Remember that the Jesus Prayer is a mental prayer without images. The icons are intended to create only a personal sacred space, an environment for silence and solitude — not for the Jesus Prayer itself.

Consider in this regard the instruction of St. Ignatius Brianchaninov:

> Holy icons are accepted by the Holy Church for the inspiration of pious remembrances and feelings, but never for the inflaming of imagination during prayer. As you stand before the icon of Christ, stand as if you are before the Lord Jesus Christ himself, who is everywhere present in his divinity and physically present before you in his icon. When you stand before the icon of the Mother of God, stand as though before the very all-holy Virgin, but keep your mind without images. There is a great difference between being in the Lord's

---

210 See *Publicans Prayer Book*, 3rd ed. (Boston: Sofia Press, 2017). One of the Little Hours is recommended for this purpose.

presence and imagining him directly. The experience of the Lord's presence brings the soul into a salvific sense of awe and feeling of reverence, while imagining the form of Christ and his saints burdens the mind with a kind of carnality and brings it into a false, proud high opinion of itself. The soul is lead into a false sense of delusion.[211]

c. Ask Jesus to guide your efforts, offering him your time and telling him your desire to enter more deeply into relationship with him, to have him as the center of your life. This is personal time devoted to him and him alone.

d. Become comfortable in the desired position such as sitting during the prayer, become centered and focused, begin the rhythmic breathing, and slowly begin the words of the Jesus Prayer.

e. Beware of distractions such as ticking clocks and pets. Secure them in a separate room.

5. **When should I practice the Jesus Prayer? How long should I pray?**

a. Finding time for prayer always seems difficult. Each person needs to determine the best time of day, generally one that is conducive for consistency. One practitioner indicated his designated time is 3 a.m. when the house is as silent as it can ever be and everyone else is asleep.

b. Avoid unnecessary distractions. For example, dedicate the

---

211 Brianchaninov, *The Field*, 143-144.

immediate waking moment to the Lord—the best time. Do not check the iPhone or Internet, both of which will lead to unnecessary distractions. There is enough time in the day to attend to other matters. Offer the first fruits of the day to the Lord; allow Jesus to be the center of your life. Make him the priority.

As St. Ignatius Brianchaninov advised, "When you rise from sleep, let your first thought be of God. Bring God the very beginning of your thoughts before they have been spoiled by any worldly impressions."[212]

c. The amount of time allotted to prayer is up to the individual. The recommendation is to make it consistent—the same time each day. In the spiritual guide, *The Art of Prayer,* St. Theophan the Recluse recommends that at the beginning, an allotted time must be given to the prayer in order to become deeply rooted[213] and later mentions half an hour, an hour, or more, acknowledging it is hard at first.[214] Another spiritual guide, *Unseen Warfare,* tells us: "Only do not undertake too much at first, but increase the number of repetitions gradually as your *enjoyment* of the prayer grows."[215] Consistency and practice are the keys. "The worth of one's prayer is not merely a question of quantity, but of quality."[216]

d. Some practitioners rely on their prayer ropes to designate the end of the prayer period. Others set an alarm. This

---

212 Ibid., 138.

213 *The Art of Prayer: An Orthodox Anthology,* compiled by Igumen Chariton of Valamo, ed. Timothy Ware, transl. by E. Kadloubovsky and E.M. Palmer (London: Faber & Faber, 1997), 154.

214 Ibid., 162.

215 *Unseen Warfare,* being the "Spiritual Combat" and "Path to Paradise" of Lorenzo Scupoli, ed. Nicodemus of the Holy Mountain, revised by Theophan the Recluse, translated by E. Kadloubovsky and G.E.H. Palmer (London: Faber and Faber, 1963), 160. Emphasis added by the author.

216 Evagrius Ponticus, *De Oratione* 151. Taken from Bunge, *Earthen Vessels,* 120.

is really at the discretion of the individual. However, better to set an alarm than to be constantly distracted during prayer, wondering how much time has elapsed or wondering if you will be late.

e.   Metropolitan Kallistos Ware of Diokleia reminds us that the Jesus Prayer can be done at any time of the day. He says, for example, that before any conversation he recites the Jesus Prayer twice to "elevate the conversation."[217] When stress or concerns arise, a brief recitation of the prayer can be an antidote. Many practitioners suggest establishing a daily period for the Prayer, such as a fixed time in the morning, and then returning to the prayer throughout the day, perhaps before a meeting, or while waiting for a computer to boot, or when encountering stressful situations like delays in traffic.

f.   Simply make time each day for the Jesus Prayer. As a theology professor from St. Meinrad Seminary said: "Until you are convinced that prayer is the best use of your time, you will not have time for prayer."[218] It is worth making time to encounter the Divine Presence dwelling within each of us.

6.   What is a Rule of Prayer, and why is it important?

Each person should have a Rule of Prayer. As St. Ignatius Brianchaninov advised, "Choose a rule for yourself in accordance within your own strength."[219] A Rule of Prayer consists of practices to follow daily, such as morning and evening prayer, time for contemplation, liturgy; the rule may

---

217   Metropolitan Kallistos Ware, "A Lecture on the Jesus Prayer," presented on June 22, 2012 in St. John the Baptist Cathedral (ROCOR), Washington, DC. http://myocn.net/metropolitan-kallistos-ware-jesus-prayer/.

218   Fr. Hiliary Ottensmeyer, quoted in Guerric DeBona, OSB, *Preaching Effectively, Revitalizing Your Church* (New York/Mahwah, NJ: Paulist Press, 2009), 29.

219   Brianchaninov, *The Refuge*, 146.

identify the time of day for these practices. The purpose of the rule is to help a person grow spiritually. Accordingly, it should not be so burdensome that it is difficult to complete on a daily basis. Nor should it become a heroic effort that later becomes a source of pride that is used to criticize others who may have a lesser rule. The key is to adopt something that can be done daily. A monastic, for example, has more time to devote to prayer than a lay person. However, each should have a rule. As Brianchaninov advised:

> Having chosen for yourself a prayer rule that accords to your strength and spiritual needs, try to diligently and constantly fulfill it. This is necessary to uphold the moral strength of your soul, just as the body's strength needs sustaining by daily, healthy food eaten at appointed times.[220]

7. What are the best preparatory steps for prayer?

Here are some practical suggestions from St. Ignatius Brianchaninov:

a. Start with a stomach that is not too full.

b. Set aside all earthly cares that may cause distractions.

c. Forgive all offenses with sincerity of heart.

d. Show gratitude to God for all sorrowful events.

e. Abandon reverie and absentmindedness.

f. Have reverent fear.[221]

---

220 Ibid., 146-47.
221 Ibid., 134.

As one anonymous Athonite monk wrote:

> Our Lord Jesus Christ, the Heavenly King, who is pure and beyond all purity, does not simply and by chance enter into a heart that is imprudent, unprepared, and filthy, for it is said, "God does not enter into an imprudent heart. But if he does enter, he departs quickly."[222]

He added:

> The preparation of the heart consists of the following: constant fasting, countless hardships of the body, and extreme humility. Constant fasting cleanses the body of the faster from the workings and substance of evil desire, while bodily hardships mortify and deaden the unruly surges of the flesh. Extreme humility brings the prayer to the person …[223]

Note that such preparation is in addition to repentance and forgiveness, previously discussed above.

8. Interior stillness is hard! What should I do?

Yes, it is. However, remember the Four "R's" (Resist, Retain, Return, and no Regret). It does take practice and discipline. As St. John of Karpathos wrote in a seventh century letter:

> A great effort and much toil are needed in

---

222 A Monk of Mount Athos, *The Watchful Mind*, 36.
223 Ibid.

prayer before we can reach a state in which
our mind is no longer troubled, and so attain
the inward heaven of the heart where Christ
dwells. As St. Paul says, 'Do you not realize
that Christ dwells within you.....'[224]

Related to attentiveness to prayer is absentmindedness,
which is a thief of prayer. Praying in a half-baked or distracted
manner will not bear fruit. Remember, too, that seemingly
good thoughts that arise in prayer are distractions or delusions.
As St. Ignatius Brianchaninov advised:

Reject all apparently good thoughts and all
apparently bright reasoning that come to you
during prayer, distracting you from prayer.
They come from the realm of falsely named
wisdom, and they sit astride vanity, riders on
a horse.[225]

A lay person related these experiences with the Jesus
Prayer:

In my person experience, quieting the mind is
still the hardest part to accomplish. The image I
have in my head is one of loading up a backpack
with everything I want to take to God: Prayers,
intentions for others, needs for my children and
myself, my family and friends, gratitude for
blessings, etc. I fill the backpack *full*. Then, as I
walk to my quiet place to enter my inner room,
I have to take off the backpack, set it down in

---

224 St. John of Karpathos, "For the Encouragement of the Monks in India Who had written to
    Him: One Hundred Texts." Taken from *The Philokalia: The Complete Text*, vol. I, transl.
    G.E.H. Palmer, P. Sherrard, and K. Ware (London: Faber & Faber, 1979), 310.
225 Brianchaninov, *The Refuge*, 138.

the hallway, walk into my room, and close the door. I leave the backpack outside, leaving it at the foot of the cross, and then walk into the classroom of silence.

When we enter the inner room, God already knows our deepest thoughts and needs and desires. He already knows what we are asking for and are thankful for. So, we do not need to ask. What we need is to invoke the Name of Jesus, acknowledging him as the Son of God, asking him for mercy—humbly and undeserved of his great love for us.[226]

This is an excellent example of trusting in God to take care of our needs, while we spend time with him in silence. Recall Mother Teresa's philosophy: Pray and trust.

9. Is the Jesus Prayer worth the effort?

Practitioners note that their lives are more in sync when they actively practice the Jesus Prayer. Remember, the intention of the Jesus Prayer is to encounter Jesus, to experience his Divine Presence and enter more deeply into relationship with him—*nothing else.* Accordingly, we take solace in the fact that God knows our intentions and is pleased even when we feel our own efforts are not bearing fruit. Recall the lesson of the five loaves and two fish.[227] We provide all we have and allow God to make up the difference. Remember, too, the

---

226 Private reflections by a practitioner of the Jesus Prayer shared with the author.
227 See Matt. 14:17, Mark 6:38, Luke 9:13, and John 6:9. All four Gospels contain the account of the multiplication of the five loaves and two fish. As written in the Gospel of John, "There is a boy here who has five barley loaves and two fish; but what good are these for so many?" In this case, it was enough to feed 5,000. It is the same with our prayer. We offer all that we have and depend upon God to supply the difference.

Parable of the Persistent Widow and the need to pray without becoming weary.[228] As Elder Porphyrios wrote:

> When Christ enters your heart, your life changes. Christ is everything. Whoever experiences Christ within himself, experiences ineffable things—holy and sacred things. He lives in exultation. These things are true. People have experienced them—hermits on the Holy Mountain (Mount Athos). Continually and with longing they whisper the prayer: 'Lord Jesus Christ ...'[229]

The fruits of prayer will ultimately manifest themselves in other places in our lives: our relationship with family and with others, in the service we render (think of Mother Teresa and the Missionaries of Charity), and in our daily disposition ("The Joy of the Gospel fills the hearts and lives of all who encounter Jesus"). The Jesus Prayer is a spiritual discipline intended to create warmth of heart, love of God, which in turn manifests itself in love of neighbor. Ultimately, everything we do flows forth and is guided by this deep interior relationship with the Divine Presence dwelling within us. Everything we do becomes an extension of our relationship with God. In *The Pilgrim's Way,* the peasant seeks to find the meaning of St. Paul's instruction to "pray without ceasing."[230] A monastic elder whom he meets explains:

> I say frequent prayer because purity and perfection in prayer is not within our reach, as St. Paul the Apostle indicates. The Spirit comes

---

228 Cf. Luke 18:1.
229 Elder Porphyrios, *Wounded by Love*, 99.
230 1 Thess. 5:17.

to help us in our weakness when we do not know how to pray.[231] Consequently, our only contribution toward perfection in prayer, the mother of all spiritual good, is regularity and constancy. "If you win the mother, you will have the children also," says Isaac the Syrian. Acquire the habit of prayer and it will be easy for you to do good. This basic truth is not clearly understood or presented by those who are lacking practical experience and who are not acquainted with the mystical teachings of the holy Fathers.[232]

We trust our Heavenly Father to provide us with our daily bread. He will grant us his grace when and as we need it, because he alone knows what we need. This might include the grace to endure difficult circumstances or situations in life. We are not spared the crosses in our daily lives, for Jesus tells us, "If anyone wishes to come after me, he must deny himself and take up his cross daily and follow me."[233] Like the Paralytic at the Pool of Siloam, we are given the strength to lift up our burdens rather than be paralyzed by them. Recall Mother Teresa's simple philosophy: "pray and trust." The order is important because it is hard to trust someone without knowing him. Thus, prayer is one of the ways we encounter Jesus, coming to know the Divine Presence within, and gaining the courage to surrender ourselves to the Divine Will.

Jesus will not remove our burdens. He did not ascend the cross so we would be spared a similar fate. "Christ suffered so

---

231 Rom. 8:26.
232 *The Way of a Pilgrim and the Pilgrim Continues His Way,* transl. Helen Bacovcin (New York: Image Books Doubleday, 1978) 17-8.
233 Luke 9:23.

that we could handle suffering with him."[234] We are fortunate that we have a most excellent guide who not only showed us the way through his own example, but who remains with us to guide us on our journey—if we allow him to enter our hearts. "This is why for Christians the joyful faith in the Risen One never loses sight of the Crucified One."[235] As St. Ignatius Brianchaninov wrote, "Come to understand that the sufferings sent to you are for your well-being."[236]

We can be assured that at various times in our lives our faith will be tested by storms. Is our house of faith built upon rock or sand?[237] We will also encounter temptation. The irony is "the demons fight hardest when God is near; the darkness of the shadow is in direct proportion to the brilliance of the light."[238] The closer we remain to Christ, with him at the center of our lives, the greater our strength and courage to weather any adverse situation. This is because if we have implicit trust, God will grant us the grace we need to endure. "In the grievous warfare with the invisible enemies of our salvation, our best weapon is the Jesus Prayer."[239]

As St. Ignatius Brianchaninov advised:

Let us not fear, practitioners of the Jesus Prayer, neither winds nor storms! Winds are demonic thoughts and images; storms are the agitations of the passions, aroused by those thoughts and images. From the midst of the fiercest storm, with constancy, courage, and weeping, let us

---

234 Gabe Martini, "Carrying the Cross and Suffering in Hope," *On Behalf of All* online. *http://onbehalfofall.org/carrying-the-cross-and-suffering-in-hope*.
235 Laird, *Into the Silent Land*, 119.
236 Brianchaninov, *The Refuge*, 185.
237 See Matt. 7:24-27.
238 John Chryssavgis, *In the Heart of the Desert: The Spirituality of the Desert Fathers and Mothers* (Bloomington, IN: World Wisdom, Inc., 2003), xii.
239 Brianchaninov, *The Refuge*, 201.

cry out to the Lord Jesus Christ. He will forbid the winds and the waves, and we, having come to know the might of Jesus from experience, will offer him worthy worship: "Truly, you are the Son of God" (Matt. 14:33). We battle for our salvation. Our eternal faith depends on our victory or our defeat.[240]

There is power in the name of Jesus. We need to hold our ground.

10. Why is there such a focus on humility?

The Jesus Prayer is built on humble recognition of who each of us are, "a sinner." It is an acknowledgment of the brokenness in our own lives and within humanity as a whole. When reading the *Sayings of the Desert Fathers*, there is a constant focus on the sinful nature and humility of "unprofitable servants."[241] As Abba Tithoes said, think of oneself "as inferior to all creatures."[242] Other spiritual fathers, such as St. Seraphim of Sarov, emphasize this as well. St. Ignatius Brianchaninov wrote:

> Humility is the only altar on which we are allowed by the spiritual law to bring the sacrifice of prayer. From this altar table, our service of prayer can ascend to God and appear before his face. Humility is the only vessel from which the hand of God places his gifts of grace.[243]

---

240 Ibid, 207.
241 See Luke 17:10. "When you have done all you have been commanded, say, 'We are unprofitable servants; we have done what we were obliged to do.'"
242 *Sayings of the Desert Fathers*, 237.
243 Brianchaninov, *The Refuge*, 260.

This foundation of humility is very important. Reflect carefully on the Parable of the Publican and the Pharisee.[244] "But the tax collector stood at a distance and would not even raise his eyes to heaven, but beat his breast and prayed, 'O God, be merciful to me a sinner.'"[245] Jesus concluded this parable with a clear statement: "I tell you, the latter (tax collector/ publican) went home justified, not the former (Pharisee); for everyone who exalts himself will be humbled, and the one who humbles himself will be exalted."[246]

Consider the advice of St. Isaac the Syrian: "The Fear of God is the beginning of virtue, and it is said to be the offspring of faith."[247] Recall that per the Simple Path, the fruit of prayer is faith. Thus, our approach to God in prayer should be one of reverential awe and humility. It is also interesting to note that the parable contrasts two dispositions toward prayer and the prayer of the publican (O God, be merciful to me a sinner) becomes an integral part of the Jesus Prayer: *Lord Jesus Christ, Son of God, have mercy on me, a sinner.*

The reality is that we are all broken individuals, this brokenness manifesting itself in different ways: suffering, temptations, addictions, separation from loved ones, separation from God, despair. We are broken as a society when one considers our consumeristic "throw-away" mentality, attempts to create various "pecking orders," focus on individual achievement and gratification without regarding the toll on others, and so forth. Pope St. John Paul II described these as the "seeds of disunity." So, whether we are experiencing a personal desert at this very moment or not, we are all likely experiencing some brokenness in our lives. Part of the reason to enter into

---

244 See Luke 18:9-14.
245 Luke 18:13.
246 Luke 18:14.
247 *The Ascetical Homilies of Saint Isaac the Syrian,* 113. Homily One.

a deeper relationship with Christ, to experience his Divine Presence, is to come to terms with our brokenness, in essence, to confront our humanity. We are not equal to God. We do not create God in our own image. He is Creator, and we are his creatures, flawed and broken, with a vast divide between us. Yet despite our failings, God desires to share his abundant life with us, sending his own Son to show us the way. "[T]o those who accepted him he gave the power to become children of God, to those who believe in his name."[248]

The Desert Fathers and Mothers were convinced that all one had to do was to cry out to our merciful Father, who so loved humanity that he gave us his only Son to die for us in order that we might once again have eternal life.[249] God's forgiving mercy was deemed freely available, as long as we were willing to cry out to God with sincerity. He would do the rest. St. John Chrysostom (347-407) would frequently say in his homilies: "Have you sinned? Tell God: 'I have sinned.' Is that difficult?"[250] St. Theophan the Recluse insisted that to admit, "I am a sinner" is more important than just saying, "I have sinned."[251] This creates the conviction of the necessity of confessing a constant state of being locked into sin as sinners and of always needing the mercy of God, a mercy that will be readily granted to those who cry out to God and acknowledge their brokenness.[252]

As we enter into silent prayer, we learn to yield to the Indwelling Divine Presence of Jesus Christ, the Divine Physician, who alone can bring life, and in abundance.[253] We

---

248 John 1:12.
249 See Jn. 3:16.
250 St. John Chrysostom. *De Paenitentia* 2.2, PG 49, 285. Taken from Maloney, *Prayer of the Heart*, 92.
251 Tomáš Špidlík, SJ, "La doctrine spirituelle de Théophane le Reclus," *Orientalia Christiana Analecta*, Series 172 (Rome: Pontifical Oriental Institute, 1965), 147. Cited in Maloney. *Prayer of the Heart*, 92.
252 See Maloney, *Prayer of the Heart*, 92.
253 See John 10:10.

cry out as often as we can, day and night, with distrust in our own power to save ourselves, but with childlike trust in Jesus the Healer: *Lord, Jesus Christ, Son of God, have mercy on me, a sinner.* This demands a life of reflection, of experiencing the light of God's Indwelling Divine Presence, and his infinite love. In his light we see our darkness.

In that darkness, we honestly recognize our guilt and sinfulness. We move far beyond mere actions to understand, by the power of the Holy Spirit, our brokenness and constant need of God's forgiving, healing love. The deeper our sorrow through the Spirit's illumination, the stronger our wish to freely surrender to our all-powerful, all-merciful God. We die to self-centeredness through interior weeping in order to rise to a new life in the Risen Jesus Christ.[254]

Through our entry into silence and solitude, through our innermost prayer of the heart, we experience our interior brokenness and alienation from God. We will often find a hardness of heart built up through years of bitterness, complacency, pride, and indifference to God's call to share in his divine life. However, as we proceed in our journey to come into greater touch with God's presence, the Divine Presence that dwells within us, we may experience the replacement of a heart of stone with a heart of flesh.[255]

Lord Jesus Christ, Son of God, have mercy on me, a sinner.

11. I have tried the Jesus Prayer, and it just doesn't work for me! Now what?

There is a reason prayer is called a *discipline.* Just like playing a musical instrument or excelling in athletics, prayer

---

254 Maloney, *Prayer of the Heart,* 96-97.
255 See Ezek. 36:26.

requires rigor and discipline. Do not despair and do not give up. As written in the classic work *Unseen Warfare*:

> Do not set a time for achievement in this prayer. Decide only one thing: to work, and to work. Months and years will go by before the first feeble indications of success begin to show. One of the Mount Athos fathers said of himself that two years of work passed before his heart grew warm. With another father this warmth came after eight months. With each man it comes in accordance with his powers and his diligence in this work.[256]

In our 5G, high-speed Internet world, with its instant access to information, we have come to expect immediate results—and grow impatient when they do not happen. However, there is no accelerating the experiences of the Jesus Prayer except by faithfully practicing it and allowing God's grace to manifest itself in our lives. Part of God's lesson is to surrender ourselves to him, to place faith in the plan he has for each of us, even if it does not happen in the timeframe or manner in which we expect. God works in his time frame, not ours—and this is part of our spiritual growth. The practice of the Jesus Prayer is no different—God will provide what we need when we need it. Patient perseverance is part of the deal.

The Jesus Prayer, like the spiritual journey, has its ups and downs. One monk compared it to the children's game, "Chutes and Ladders." Sometimes we are climbing and other times we are sliding backward. The key, as in any relationship, is fidelity. It is not important to God whether we achieve perfect prayer, which is impossible. More important to him is

---

256 *Unseen Warfare,* 161.

whether we have been faithful to our prayer discipline (Rule of Prayer). Patient waiting is a necessary aspect of prayer. As St. Ignatius Brianchaninov advised, "When you feel dryness or insensibility, do not abandon your prayer."[257] As St. Anna Schäffer (1882-1925) said, "Jesus will sometimes test us as to whether we are persevering." This is like gold tested in fire,[258] or the removal of all that weakens our foundation of faith.[259]

It takes time to remove the clutter that has accumulated in our hearts. We have filled ourselves with love for the world, and it requires great persistence to allow Jesus to help us overcome the world[260] and fill our hearts with his presence. We have the examples of many spiritual fathers and mothers who have gone before us and who have attested to the joy and peace of a heart filled with Christ.

So, the question we must ask ourselves is whether we want to continue chasing after the world and all its empty promises—remaining disillusioned and unfulfilled—or if we want Christ to fill our hearts. God gave humanity the freedom to choose. Virtually all who traveled the spiritual road before would advise on the need for patient endurance and persistence. We need to cultivate and nurture the seed planted in us so it can sprout, grow, develop deep roots, and bear fruit that will last. If we ease up or become complacent, we will not reap the fruit. We cannot be half-baked or absentminded; we need to be all in. We need to take our

257 Brianchaninov, The Refuge, 137.
258 See Wis. 3:1, 6. ""The souls of the righteous are in the hand of God, and no torment shall touch them. As gold in the furnace, he proved them, and as sacrificial offerings he took them to himself."
259 See Matt. 7:24-25. "Everyone who listens to these words of mine and acts on them will be like a wise man who built his house on rock. The rain fell, the floods came, and the winds came and buffeted the house. But it did not collapse; it had been set solidly on rock."
260 See John 16:33. "I have told you this so that you might have peace in me. In the world you will have trouble, but take courage, I have conquered the world."

relationship with God seriously if we desire a personal relationship with him.

Most Spiritual Fathers and Mothers describe the struggle associated with prayer. God wants us to be completely committed, not giving up when journey becomes difficult. It is about complete surrender to him, which is difficult given our inherent human tendency toward selfishness and self-reliance. So we will struggle, we will experience times of spiritual dryness in our prayer, and we will find ourselves tempted to give up. If we choose to persevere, God will give us the graces we need. Attentiveness in prayer and compunction are gifts of the Holy Spirit.[261] However, along the way, God will grant us a few hints where we can experience his presence, the sweetness of inner peace, which provides us with a reminder of the fruit that our labor can produce. As St. Ignatius Brianchaninov explained, "The experience of God's presence is a very high state!"[262]

He further teaches:

> In the zealot, flourishing prayer begins at first to reveal itself through a special active attentiveness—from time to time, the mind is unexpectedly taken by it and bound to the words of the prayer. Later, this state becomes more constant and longer lasting: the mind somehow attaches itself to the words of the prayer, and through them is united to the heart.[263]

---

261 Cf. Brianchaninov, *The Field*, 144.
262 Ibid., 144.
263 Ibid.

Thus, he reminds us that the fruit of prayer cannot be produced by human initiative alone. God cannot be manipulated nor deceived. Rather, the fruit of prayer is granted through human-divine collaboration (*synergeia*) and we must prove our desire to truly want our relationship with God above all else. That is why there will be struggles, proof of our ongoing and unwavering desire. Brianchaninov also noted, "Do not search for exalted experiences in prayer—they are not proper to a sinner."[264] Using again the analogy of the vessel to be filled by divine grace, we must continuously work on purifying our hearts and minds of all that would create obstacles in our relationship with God. We have to come to an understanding of our sinful nature and constantly strive to overcome it. More will be said about this in the next chapter.

Brianchaninov provided some additional insights with regard to the fruit of prayer:

> The feelings that arise from prayer and repentance consist of a clean conscience, a calm soul, peace with all your near ones and contentment with the circumstances of life, mercy and co-suffering toward all men, abstinence from all passions, coldness toward the world, submission to God, and strength during the fight with sinful thoughts and inclinations. With such feelings, in which one can foretaste salvation, you should be content. Do not seek exalted spiritual states or prayerful ecstasy before their time. They are not as you imagine them to be—the activity of the Holy Spirit, who gives high

---

264 Ibid., 145.

states of prayer, is not comprehensible to the worldly mind.[265]

Should we choose to earnestly pursue the spiritual life, the prayer, with great practice and consistency, will become rooted in our hearts, even when we are not conscious of it. On each breath or beat of the heart, the Jesus Prayer continues, thus creating a warmth of heart spoken of by the Spiritual Fathers.[266] Through this effort, we enter into an ever deepening relationship with God, preparing ourselves for our ultimate destiny of union with him in heaven.

12. What is the importance of having a Spiritual Father (Spiritual Direction)?

Many of the spiritual masters advise that practitioners of the Jesus Prayer should have a Spiritual Father or Mother to provide the necessary guidance along the way. Ideally, we will have a spiritual guide for the journey and would encourage all those who want to go deeper into the Jesus Prayer to find one. Patriarch Callistus of Constantinople and Ignatius of Xanthopoulos were Athonite monks of the fourteenth century and wrote in their instructions:

> To this end, spare no effort in trying to find a teacher and guide ...; he should be a man bearing the Spirit within him, leading a life corresponding to his words, lofty in vision of mind, humble in thought of himself, of good disposition in everything, and generally such

---

265 Ibid.
266 Cf. *Unseen Warfare,* 185-191, "On Warmth of Heart." Specifically, it is written: "Spiritual warmth of heart is the fruit of feeling for God and for everything divine" (185). "Cooling of the heart is produced by a weakening of attention caused by temptations, worldly surroundings, or by wiles of the enemy who contrives to induce a man to come out of his inner self"(187).

as a teacher of Christ should be, according to Divine words.

Having found such a man, cleave to him with body and spirit like a devoted son to his father and from then onwards obey all his commands implicitly, accord with him everything, and see him not as a mere man, but as Christ himself.[267]

However, because finding such a guide may not always be possible in this day and age, here are some suggestions as to what can be done in the absence of spiritual direction:

a. Consider confession, at least monthly if not even more frequently (e.g., weekly). Strive to confess everything sincerely and exactly.[268]

b. Consider one's relationships with family and colleagues. The quality of human relationships is an unerring guide to the quality of one's prayer. As St. Seraphim of Sarov said: "Learn to be peaceful, and thousands around you will find salvation."[269] How are you dealing, not only with family and friends, but difficult people or strangers who come your way? Do you recognize Christ in his most distressing disguises?

The reality is that most of us have habits or demons with which we regularly struggle. These could be impatience, judgment of others, pride, arrogance, anger, vanity, despair, or impure thoughts or fantasies.

---

267 The Monks Callistus and Ignatius of Xanthopoulos, "Directions to Hesychasts." Taken from *Writings from the Philokalia on Prayer of the Heart*, transl. E. Kadloubovsky and G.E.H. Palmer (London: Faber and Faber, 1992), 174.
268 See Ibid., 177.
269 Zander, *St. Seraphim of Sarov*, x.

For example, if we struggle with impatience, do we find ourselves becoming more patient, say, with difficult people or in circumstances such as heavy traffic? If we struggle with judgment of others, are we becoming more tolerant? Over time, we should see evidence of transformation, albeit often slow, painful, and incremental. We will still stumble and fall. The spiritual journey is one of constant struggle.

c. Consider regular reflection on the Gospels and the messages of Jesus, both in his teachings and actions, and how this applies to our own spiritual formation.[270] How is God speaking to me through the Scriptures?

d. Consider the wisdom of the Holy Fathers and past spiritual elders through reading. Some examples to consider are:

- *The Sayings of the Desert Fathers.*

- St. John Climacus, *The Ladder of Divine Ascent.*

- St. Symeon the New Theologian, *The Discourses.*

- St. Nil Sorsky, *The Complete Works.*

- St. Seraphim of Sarov.[271]

- St. Nicodemos of the Holy Mountain, *A Handbook of Spiritual Counsel.*

- St. Ignatius Brianchaninov, *The Field* and *The Refuge.*

---

270 An overview of these lessons can be found in the work, Edward Kleinguetl, *Choosing Life in Christ: A Vocation to Holiness* (Parker, CO: Outskirts Press, 2019), Conference No. 3, "Formation."

271 We recommend starting with Valentine Zander, *St. Seraphim of Sarov*, transl. Sr. Gabriel Anne, SSC (Crestwood, NY: St. Vladimir's Seminary Press, 1976).

- St. Theophan the Recluse, *The Path to Salvation* and *The Spiritual Life.*

- St. John of Kronstadt, *My Life in Christ* (2013 edition).

- Elder Joseph the Hesychast, *Monastic Wisdom.*

- St. Silouan the Athonite.[272]

- St. Paisios of Mount Athos, *Spiritual Counsels* (five volumes to date).

- The classic, *The Pilgrim's Tale.*

- Composite works such as *Unseen Warfare*, *The Art of Prayer*, compiled by Igumen Charitan of Valamo, and selections from the *Philokalia.*[273]

- *The Ascetical Homilies of Saint Isaac the Syrian.* Many Holy Fathers quote him, considering him a source *par excellence* in the spiritual life. We included this last on the list because as St. Paul writes, "I fed you milk, not solid food, because you were unable to take it."[274] Thus, we too start with "milk," whereas the writings of St. Isaac are very rich fare.

---

272 We recommend Archimandrite Sophrony Sakharov, *St. Silouan the Athonite*, transl. Rosemary Edmonds (Crestwood, NY: St. Vladimir's Seminary Press, 1991). Elder Sophrony was a disciple of St. Silouan for many years.

273 See *The Pilgrim's Tale*, 81-82. In this story, the elder advises the pilgrim as to the order in which to read the *Philokalia*. He suggests: "First read the book of Nicephorus the Monk, in part 2; second, the book of Gregory of Sinai, except for the brief chapters; third, Symeon the New Theologian's 'On the Three Modes of Prayer,' and 'A Discourse on Faith;' fourth, the book of Kallistos and Ignatios. These fathers' work contain the full explanation, directions, and doctrine concerning the interior prayer of the heart. Anyone can understand them. If, however, you desire an even clearer instruction on prayer, look in part 4 for the 'Abbreviated Description of the Mode of Prayer' by his holiness Kallistos, patriarch of Constantinople." There is a separate book entitled, *Writings from the Philokalia on Prayer of the Heart*, transl. E. Kadloubovsky and G.E.H. Palmer (London: Faber and Faber, 1992), which contains all these recommended texts attributed to the elder in Part 1. This is a separate book from the four volumes of the *Philokalia* currently in print.

274 1 Cor. 3:2.

Some initial suggestions are provided in the section entitled, "Recommended Further Reading and Reference."

e. Consider regular retreats to rest, reflect, and renew oneself in the spiritual life. Ideally, such a retreat is annual, generally for a full weekend or at least a full day. It is important take a pause from day-to-day routines to focus on our lives in Christ, recommitting ourselves to the spiritual journey.

f. Consider pilgrimages to holy sites or monasteries; a pause from the daily routine and a chance to reflect on various Spiritual Fathers and Mothers.

13. How can the Jesus Prayer experience be enhanced?

It is important to keep in mind that prayer is a single, albeit important, element of The Art of Spiritual Life and is the foundation of faith.[275] However, it cannot be separated from other elements of the spiritual life such as fasting, struggling through ascetical practices, participating in the sacramental life of the Church (especially Repentance and Eucharist), being nurtured through Sacred Scripture especially the Gospels, and gaining insights through other spiritual reading. Thus, the fullness of the spiritual life is based on a combination of elements. With this in mind, people often ask how they can enhance their experiences associated with the Jesus Prayer. Consider these suggestions:

a. Repentance is essential to our relationship with God. Consider more frequent participation in the Holy Mystery of Repentance (Sacrament of Reconciliation). The more we strive to be in relationship with God, the

---

275 The fruit of silence is prayer, the fruit of prayer is faith.

more the demons will try to disrupt that relationship. We will experience temptations and struggles. They can easily come through small sins such as gossip, pride, selfishness, and being judgmental—sins that seem to simply creep in if we are not attentive. The small sins can easily become habits and can ultimately cause a contraction of our hearts. There is a strong belief that these smaller encroachments need to be kept in check, not allowing poisonous seeds to take root in our hearts.[276] Thus, there is a great emphasis on the need to seek the Holy Mystery of Repentance (Confession) on a more frequent basis.

As Pope Francis writes: "The confessional must not be a torture chamber, but an *encounter* with the Lord's mercy which spurs us on to do our best."[277] Said simply, being in communion with God, recognizing his Divine Presence in ourselves and in others, is easier when one remains reconciled with him, recognizing our weaknesses and regularly seeking his mercy. After all, this is our prayer: Lord Jesus Christ, Son of God, have *mercy* on me, a sinner. Eastern Spiritual Fathers write often about the need for repentance and even the gift of tears to mourn our sins. Frequency for receiving the Holy Mystery (Sacrament) is up to the individual. However, regular participation in the Holy Mystery will allow us to experience healing and wholeness in our relationship with the Divine.

---

276 See *Catechism of the Catholic Church*, 2nd.Ed. Revised in accordance with the official Latin text promulgated by Pope John Paul II (Rome: Libreria Editrice Vaticana, 1997), 457. Discusses the proliferation of sin, similar to the concerns in the Eastern Churches: "Sin creates a proclivity to sin; it genders vice by repetition of the same acts. This results in perverse inclinations, which cloud conscience and corrupt the concrete judgment of good and evil. Thus, sin tends to reproduce itself and reinforce itself, but it cannot destroy the moral sense at its root." No. 1865.

277 Pope Francis, *Evangelii Gaudium,* no. 44.

In his Pastoral Letter for Christmas 2019, His Grace Bishop Milan Lach, SJ discusses the importance of making ready to receive Christ, and in particular, before receiving the Holy Gifts—the Eucharist at liturgy. Thus, he states that if we desire "to receive the real Christ in the Eucharist every Sunday, we should go to holy confession at least once per month. Otherwise, we are receiving the Holy Gifts unworthily and we are risking our salvation."[278]

b. Related to more frequent participation in the Holy Mystery of Repentance is a nightly examination of conscience. This is required of Roman Church clergy in the Office of Night Prayers. However, it is good practice for everyone to examine his or her relationship with God and others daily, monitoring our weaknesses and failings, and preventing poisonous weeds from becoming widespread in our hearts. There are beautiful "Prayers before Sleep" in the *Publicans Prayer Book*[279] that can be recited and used as a basis for reflection. Consider how the enemy sows weeds in the Parable of the Weeds among the Wheat.[280] The Spiritual Fathers say we must maintain constant vigilance. The Greek term used is *nepsis* (Νιψις), which means sober vigilance or spiritual attentiveness. The analogy of this would be an alert guard in a watchtower at the entrance to our hearts, allowing no impure thoughts or evil desires to pass. Complacency or lack of constant attention weakens our defenses and places our hearts at risk.

c. The Eucharist is the source and summit of the Christian

---

278 Bishop Milan Lach, SJ, "Pastoral Letter for Christmas 2019."
279 *Publicans Prayer Book*, 3rd ed. (Boston: Sofia Press, 2017).
280 See Matt. 13:24-32.

life.[281] Our starving souls need the nourishment of the Eucharist to sustain them. We need strength. Thus, we can consider more frequent reception of Eucharist as part of our ongoing spiritual formation. For example, St. John of Kronstadt encouraged daily Eucharist even for lay people. As our prayer relationship grows, so too will our longing to receive Jesus in the Holy Eucharist. Note: It goes without saying that Eucharist should always be received worthily and well, which places increased emphasis on confession.

d. Continued focus on detachment and self-denial; avoid material trappings to the fullest extent possible. This includes practices such as not eating meat on any Wednesday and Friday, even outside of Lent, and other similar practices such as regular fasting. St. John Chrysostom would tell us that fasting is one of the spiritual remedies available to us. St. Theophan the Recluse reminds us, "Where there is no prayer and fasting, there are the demons." Thus,

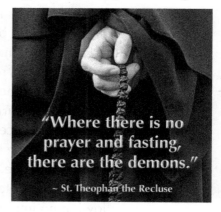

"Where there is no prayer and fasting, there are the demons."

~ St. Theophan the Recluse

many Spiritual Fathers do speak of the correlation between fasting and prayer.

e. Spiritual reading is an important way we can nourish our souls. There are two components to such reading:

281 Second Vatican Council, *Lumen Gentium,* Dogmatic Constitution of the Church (Rome: Libreria Editrice Vaticana, Nov. 21, 1964), no. 11.

Sacred Scripture and other beneficial spiritual writings.

i.   Sacred Scripture—particularly the Gospels. We need to regularly hear our Savior tell us we are precious to him (every hair on our head has been counted;[282] we are more precious than many sparrows[283]) and that that those who are burdened should come to him because he will refresh us.[284] He came to seek the lost; the lost sheep was not scolded for straying but placed lovingly on the shepherd's shoulders and returned to the fold;[285] the Prodigal Son was not scolded for his foolishness, but restored to his original dignity as a son.[286] Scripture reminds us of how much Our God truly loves us and desires us. As Elder Porphyrios advised: "Everything proceeds from Holy Scripture. You must read it continuously to learn the secrets of the spiritual struggle."[287]

ii. Other Spiritual Writings—from Ancient Church Fathers to contemporary Christian writers. Each of us can find a tradition or particular saint or particular writer whose works speak to us in a personal way.

f.   Prayer and service are not mutually exclusive. Consider the example of Mother Teresa. The warmth

---

282 Matt. 10:30.
283 Matt. 10:31.
284 Cf. Matt. 11:28.
285 See Matt. 18:12-14.
286 See Luke 15:11-32.
287 Elder Porphyrios, *Wounded by Love*, 110.

of heart created through the prayer experience can continue, manifested in acts of charity or service for neighbor (the indelible link between love of God and love of neighbor). Yet, she would tell us that all these efforts begin in silence.

14. What are the "work" and "gift" of prayer?

St. Ignatius Brianchaninov wrote:

> The work of prayer is the highest work for the human mind; the state of purity, needing no pleasant distractions, given by prayer to the mind, is the highest natural state of the mind. The ascent of the mind to God, which only begins with pure prayer, is a state beyond the natural.[288]

As with any skill, prayer can be mastered only with work, desire, and determination. God grants us the graces we need commensurate to our diligence. "The only teacher of prayer is God himself, and so true prayer is a gift of God."[289] Here is an overview of the levels of participation:

---

288 Brianchaninov, *The Field*, 148.
289 Brianchaninov, *The Refuge*, 227. He references Climacus's *Ladder*. See St. John Climacus, *The Ladder of Divine Ascent*, 281. Step 28: "On Prayer." "[Y]ou cannot discover from others the beauty of prayer. Prayer has its own special teacher in God, who 'teaches man knowledge' (Psalm 93:10). He grants the prayer of him who prays."

Level of Participation	Characteristics	Stages of Prayer per Elder Cleopa of Sihastria
Praxis	**Creating the Foundation** • Learning skills • Struggling through ascetical practices • Living the virtues • Repentance • Mourning our sins • Personal purification **Verbal Prayer** • Liturgical prayer • Psalmody • Prayers of the Church (Divine Office and prayers of the Holy Fathers (books)	Prayer of the lips – *when the prayer is just said*
Theoria	**Mental Prayer** • Contemplation • Awareness of the presence of God	Prayer of the mind – *when the prayer is comprehended* Prayer of the heart – *when the mind descends into the heart*
Pure Prayer (*kathara proseuche*)	**Prayer of the Heart** • Union with God in peace, love, and joy • Granted as gift by God; not all will achieve	Active Prayer – *when the heart starts praying alone (even in sleep)* All-Seeing Prayer – *when the unseen world becomes visible together with future, past* Ecstasy Prayer – *when the mind is taken to heaven* Contemplative Prayer – *when people can be taken to heaven*

Spiritual writers from the Western Church such as St. Teresa of Ávila have described the levels of prayer as purgative, illuminative, and unitive, which are generally comparable to our levels of participation.

As many Spiritual Fathers and Mothers advise, prayer is both "work" (the "work of prayer") and a "gift." St. Seraphim of Sarov said "acquisition of the Holy Spirit"—the gift—is the objective of prayer and the reward for the work. In the hesychast tradition, prayer requires *synergeia* (collaboration with the Divine). Jesus tells us, "Without me you can do nothing."[290] Accordingly, we do need Jesus as our guide to make progress in the spiritual life. He is "the way" and our model.

Prayer of the Heart begins with *praxis* (πρᾶξις), the process of learning skills, which involves the active struggle through ascetical practices, living the virtues, and other spiritual practices such as repentance and mourning our sins (*penthos*) to achieve personal purification. *Praxis* can lead to *theoria* (θεωρία), which is contemplation of God or a greater sense of his presence. As hesychast prayer becomes more internalized, the ultimate degree is *kathara proseuche* (καθαρή προσευχή), or pure prayer. This last degree is where the hesychast has an experience of union with God in peace, love, and joy.

To a novice, Elder Cleopa of Sihastria (1912-98) described it this way: "First pray with your voice, with words; prayer will then move from the mouth to the mind and finally to the heart. But this result requires much effort, a fountain of tears, and the grace of the Holy Spirit."[291]

---

290 John 15:5.
291 Archimandrite Ioanichie Balan, *Elder Cleopa of Sihastria*, transl. Mother Cassiana (Lake George, CO: New Varatec Publishing, 2001), 220.

Our work alone cannot "produce" prayer. Prayer is a gift granted by God in response to our work. Theologian John Breck wrote, "The quality and intensity of prayer that leads to abiding communion with God are bestowed only by the Spirit."[292] We cannot force or manipulate prayer. For example, it is reported that St. Silouan the Athonite (1866–1938) obtained the gift of pure prayer in a few days, whereas St. Symeon the New Theologian "implored God for years before he received the gift of pure prayer."[293] As advised in the famous spiritual classic *Unseen Warfare*: "Do not set a time for achievement in this prayer. Decide only one thing: to work, and to work."[294]

The Spiritual Fathers usually describe the Prayer in three stages: verbal, mental, and, finally, Prayer of the Heart. In the first stage, the prayer is repeated out loud, but quietly, which establishes a rhythm of repetition and intensity of the prayer, generally synchronized with the person's breathing. Gradually through repetition, the Prayer "seems to transcend the verbal level and root itself in the mind."[295] As mental prayer, it begins to take on a life of its own, whether the practitioner is awake or asleep, as the heart keeps watch. "Once the Prayer is imprinted on the mind, it appears to 'pray itself' spontaneously."[296] Finally, at the deepest level of prayer, *kathara proseuche* or pure prayer, the Prayer literally "descends from the mind into the heart."[297]

---

292 John Breck, "Prayer of the Heart: Sacrament of the Presence of God," *Saint Vladimir's Theological Quarterly* 29(1) (1995): 38. Consider Rom. 8:26: "For we do not know how to pray as we ought, but the Spirit itself intercedes with inexpressible groanings." This verse supports the concept of *synergeia*, human and divine collaboration.
293 Ibid., 42.
294 *Unseen Warfare: Being the Spiritual Combat and Path to Paradise of Lorenzo Scupoli*, ed. Nicodemus of the Holy Mountain, rev. Theophan the Recluse, transl. E. Kadloubovsky and G. E. H. Palmer (London: Faber and Faber, 1963), 161.
295 Breck, "Prayer of the Heart: Sacrament of the Presence of God," 41.
296 Ibid.
297 Ibid.

There, as the voice of the Spirit himself, the Prayer dwells within the inner sanctuary. It is no longer "prayed" as a conscious deliberate act, but is received, welcomed, and embraced as a manifestation of Divine Presence and life. The Prayer now associates itself with the rhythm of the heart, producing without conscious effort a ceaseless outpouring of adoration and thanksgiving. From prayer of the lips to prayer of the mind, it has become "prayer of the heart."[298]

All the great Spiritual Fathers advise that those who seek to undertake hesychast prayer should have a spiritual father or director to help guide the process. For example, an attempt to use the Prayer as a mantra or simply exploit it as a means of relaxation "will inevitably lead to spiritual shipwreck."[299] However, given the limited number of spiritual masters available today, certain books can provide guidance. These would include the writings included in the *Philokalia*, *The Pilgrim's Tale*, *The Art of Prayer*, and *Unseen Warfare*. These are considered classics. Any Christian can benefit from a genuine, pious practice of the Jesus Prayer.[300]

Not all who undertake hesychast prayer can achieve these higher levels or degrees of participation, especially that of pure prayer. Nevertheless, there is virtue in seeking the gift, whether or not it is granted, as long as it is sought out of genuine love and desire for God.[301] We can experience warmth of heart, a sense of God's presence, and experience changes within ourselves. Each of us can strive to the best of our abilities and then leave our salvation entirely in the hands of our merciful God, surrendering ourselves and aligning our will with the Divine Will.

---

298 Ibid.
299 Ibid., 39.
300 Ibid.
301 Ibid., 42.

The gift of prayer is given by God to build up the Church. While not all will achieve pure prayer, there are still fruits than can be attained by practicing prayer. These include inner peace, peaceful co-existence, and a desire to serve.

15. Is the Jesus Prayer the only form of contemplative prayer in the Church?

There are a great number of spiritual traditions and movements within the Church. Some examples include Ignatian spirituality, Franciscan spirituality, Carmelite spirituality, Opus Dei, and the Focolare Movement, just to provide a small sampling.[302] All these traditions have merit. Christians can choose the spirituality or movement in which they find themselves drawn closer to God. The Jesus Prayer was selected as our focus for these reasons:

a. The Jesus Prayer is the *oldest* of the contemplative prayer traditions, beginning with the Desert Fathers and Mothers of the third century, evolving with experience, and faithfully practiced and preserved in the Christian East until today.

b. It is the *most used* form of the contemplative prayer traditions, especially within Eastern Christian Churches, and part of the patrimony of the Universal Catholic Church via the Eastern Catholic Churches.

c. It is *based on humility,* the only tradition focusing on approaching God humbly and acknowledging who we are: sinners. Consider the Parable of the Pharisee and Publican.[303]

---

302 See http://en.wikipedia.org/wiki/Catholic_spirituality for a more detailed list of spiritual traditions and movements, to which we would also include Carthusian spirituality and Trappist spirituality. In this detailed list, the Jesus Prayer tradition (hesychast spirituality) is considered part of Desert Spirituality.

303 See Luke 18:9-14. "But the tax collector stood off at a distance and would not even raise his eyes to heaven but beat his breast and prayed, 'O God, be merciful to me a sinner.'"

d. Its *simplicity*, by asking God for the one thing we need most: *mercy*. He knows what we need before we even ask.[304] As St. Theophan the Recluse wrote:

> The practice of the Jesus Prayer is simple. Stand before the Lord with the attention in the heart, and call to him: 'Lord Jesus Christ, Son of God, have mercy on me!' The essential part of this is not the words, but in faith, contrition, and self-surrender to the Lord. With these feelings, one can stand before the Lord even without any words, and it will still be prayer.[305]

Expansion of the Heart by Focusing on the Interior Life

In summary, let us consider a perspective of St. John of Kronstadt:

> Our spiritual lives are generally divided into two conditions, distinctly different from one another. One is an expanded heart which is filled with joy and peace. The other is a contracted heart filled with fear and suffering. The causes of the first condition are the actions of the soul in conformity with the will of God. The other occurs when we go against his will.[306]

Pope Francis provides us with a similar message:

> The Joy of the Gospel fills the hearts and lives of all who encounter Jesus. Those who accept his offer of salvation are set free from sin, sorrow, inner emptiness

---

304 See Matt. 6:8.
305 *The Art of Prayer*, 89.
306 See John Iliytch Sergieff (St. John of Kronstadt), *My Life in Christ*, transl. E.E. Goulaeff (Jordanville, NY: Printshop of St. Job of Pochaev, Holy Trinity Monastery, 2000), 30.

and loneliness. With Christ joy is born constantly anew.[307]

He continues:

> Whenever our interior life becomes caught up in our own interests and concerns, there is no longer room for others, no place for the poor. God's voice is no longer heard, the quiet joy of his love is no longer felt, and the desire to do good fades[308] (in other words, contraction of the heart).

Or, there is the simple wisdom of the Desert Fathers and Mothers,[309] who are at the origins of the hesychast tradition:

> As long as a pot is on the fire, no fly nor any other animal can get near it. But as soon as it is cold, these creatures get inside. So it is for us; as long as we live lives in spiritual activities, the enemy cannot find a means of controlling us.[310]

Thus, our objective in personal prayer is to encounter the Divine Presence within, cultivating a relationship, learning to surrender to the Will of God ("Thy will be done"), and allowing our hearts to expand with love of him,[311] which in turn makes room for others. "The purer

---

307 Pope Francis, *Evangelii Gaudium*, no. 1.

308 Ibid., no. 2

309 Desert Fathers and Mothers: Though many were contemporaries of the theologians of the great Alexandrian and Antiochian Schools, they themselves were not per se theologians. They were simple people, profoundly human, and to whom we who have experienced brokenness or temptations in our lives could easily relate. Their words were not profound doctrines of faith, but simple words of wisdom from lived experience. The ascetical principles embraced by the Desert Fathers and Mothers held that the more one is rooted in God, the less one is dependent upon the transitory gifts of the earth.

310 *Sayings of the Desert Fathers*, 183. Abba Poemen.

311 See Rom. 5:5. "The love of God has been poured into our hearts through the Holy Spirit that has been given to us."

the heart is, the larger it is, and the more able it is to find room within it for a greater number of loved ones."[312] This, obviously, aligns with Jesus's description of the two greatest commandments: Love of God and the second, which is like it, love of neighbor.[313]

Returning to the Prayer throughout the Day

A lay person dedicated to the practice of the Jesus Prayer wrote a reflection on his own experiences. While he had a set time for prayer, he found himself turning to the Prayer throughout the day, reflecting a desire to return to moments of grace, the peace and stillness within. As he wrote:

- Be humble: *Lord Jesus Christ, Son of God, have mercy on me, a sinner.*

- Acknowledge our brokenness before the Lord; ask God for the grace to see ourselves as he sees us: *Lord Jesus Christ …*

- Cry out with child-like trust: *Lord Jesus Christ …*

- When your world is crumbling: *Lord Jesus Christ …*

- When you are being crushed by guilt, sorrow, sadness: *Lord Jesus Christ …*

- When darkness covers your family: *Lord Jesus Christ …*

He added:

> I believe that we can return to the Jesus Prayer at any time and offer it up to Christ, invoking His Holy Name against all evil forces, and re-centering ourselves throughout the day in the light and infinite

---

312 See St. John of Kronstadt, *My Life in Christ* (2000), 36.
313 See Matt. 22:34-40.

love of our Heavenly Father. Even when I'm not in my specific time for the Prayer, just the recitation in time of need, or at any point, creates a yearning for the deeper communion with Christ that comes from daily diligence and commitment to the Prayer.[314]

The Prayer becomes part of who we are, consistently turning to Jesus, being aware of his presence within us and our desire for him. This is how we slowly learn to surrender our will to the Divine will, recognizing that he wills for us the abundant life no matter the near-term challenges or struggles. As we learn to trust in God, we are building a true relationship with him.

Prayer without Ceasing

Many mystics have been inspired by this St. Paul passage: "Rejoice always. Pray without ceasing. In all circumstances give thanks, for this is the will of God for you in Christ Jesus."[315] Prayer without ceasing has several meanings worth considering: The simple ongoing prayer described above remaining for a time in the contemplative state and resting in the presence of the heavenly Father, and returning to the Prayer throughout the day. However, as St. Augustine of Hippo wrote:

Are we to be 'without ceasing' in bending the knee and prostrating the body and lifting up our hands, such that he says, 'without ceasing?' If that is what 'without ceasing' means, then I do not believe it is possible. There is another kind of inward prayer without ceasing, which is the *desire* of the heart.[316]

---

314 Private reflections by a practitioner of the Jesus Prayer shared with the author.
315 1 Thess. 5:16-18.
316 St. Augustine, "Commentary on the Psalms 37.14." Taken from *Colossians, 1-2 Thessalonians, 1-2 Timothy, Titus, Philemon*, ed. Peter Gorday. From Ancient Christian Commentary on Scripture, NT, vol. IX (Downers Grove, IL: InterVarsity Press, 2000), 98. Emphasis added by the author.

This desire is what the lay person, above, described when returning to the Prayer throughout the day. The Spiritual Fathers also speak of this desire by describing how the prayer continues in our heart, even when we are not conscious of it, sometimes called unconscious or self-activating prayer. As the peasant in *The Pilgrim's Tale* describes it:

> I felt that the prayer somehow was beginning to move into my heart by itself. That is, it seemed that as it beat normally my heart began to form the words of the prayer inside itself with every heartbeat; for example, at the first beat, Lord; at the second, Jesus; at the third, Christ; and so on. I stopped saying the prayer vocally and began to listen carefully to my heart speaking.[317]

With sustained practice of the Jesus Prayer, we increase the desire of our hearts for God. This increased desire is tantamount to spending more time with God, both in prayer, consciously and unconsciously, and in service to others. Question: How do we best love God? Answer: By loving those whom God loves. It is a constant, conscious realization of the presence of God no matter where we are or what we do. Desert Father Abba Moses the Black said: "If a man's deeds are not in harmony with his prayer, he labors in vain."[318] The measure of the degree of integration attained by us "must always be measured by the love and humility shown in service toward others."[319] The point is, over time as practitioners of the Jesus Prayer, hearts will be transformed, manifested in our external relationships. The more we recognize the Divine Presence within ourselves, the more we will recognize the Divine Presence within others, which draws us to love[320]

---

317 *The Pilgrim's Tale*, 68-69.
318 *Sayings of the Desert Fathers*, 141.
319 Ibid.
320 See Pope Francis, *Evangelii Gaudium*, no. 272. "Loving others is a spiritual force drawing us to union with God."

and unites us as the Body of Christ.[321] With this type of integration, an individual will gradually find inner peace and joy.

St. John Chrysostom tells us:

> Our spirit should be quick to reach out toward God, not only when it is engaged in meditation; at other times also, when it is carrying out its duties, caring for the needy, performing works of charity, giving generously in the service of others, our spirit should long for God and call him to mind, so that these works may be seasoned with the salt of God's love, and so make it a palatable offering to the Lord of the universe. Throughout the whole of our lives we may enjoy the benefit that comes from prayer if we devote a great deal of time to it.[322]

"This, too, is what Prayer of the Heart is all about."[323] It is about going forth and doing, integrating all we do and every action we take as part of our prayer experience. It does not necessarily have to be extraordinary things—picking up the house, making coffee, doing laundry—all these can be acts of ongoing prayer if done with the mindset focused on love of neighbor. As Desert Father Abba John the Dwarf said, "The foundation is our neighbor ... That is where we are to begin."[324]

For a stalk to grow or a flower to open there must be time that cannot be forced; nine months must go by for the birth of a child; to write a book or compose music often years must be dedicated to patient research. To find the mystery there must be patience, interior purification, silence, waiting.

—Pope St. John Paul II

321 See Rom. 12:5. "So we, though many, are one body in Christ and individually parts of one another."

322 St. John Chrysostom, *De Precatione*, Homily 6. Taken from *The Liturgy of the Hours*, vol. II, Office of Readings, Friday after Ash Wednesday (New York: Catholic Book Publishing Corp., 1976), 69.

323 Maloney, *Prayer of the Hearts*, 76.

324 *Sayings of the Desert Fathers*, 93.

And whatever you ask in my name, I will do, so that the Father may be glorified in the Son. If you ask anything of me in my name, I will do it.
(John 14:13-14)

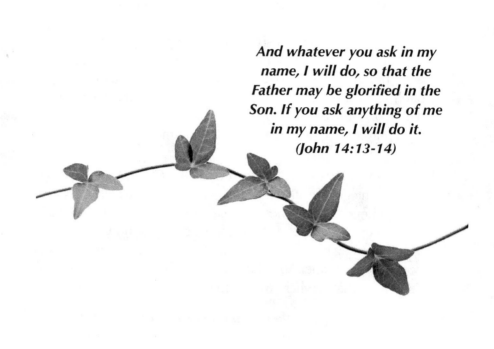

CHAPTER 5

A Foundation to the Art of Spiritual Life

"Whoever remains in me and I in him will bear much
fruit, because without me you can do nothing."
(John 15:5)

"If you want with a few words to benefit one who is eager to learn,
speak to him about prayer, right faith, and the patient acceptance of
what comes. For all else that is good is found through these."[325]
(St. Mark the Ascetic)

"The necessary, essential condition for progress in the Jesus
Prayer is living according to the commandments of the
Lord Jesus. 'Abide in My Love' (John 15:9) ..."[326]
(St. Ignatius Brianchaninov)

Opening Gospel Passage

Read: John 15:1-10 (The Vine and the Branches).

The Need for Salvation

Fundamentally, one must admit he or she is a sinner, one who is fallen. Otherwise, why would he or she seek salvation?[327] The challenge presented by the spirit of the age is one of complacency. As Cardinal Sarah writes,

---

325 St. Mark the Ascetic, "No Righteous by Works," 133.
326 Brianchaninov, *The Refuge*, 256.
327 See Ibid., 274.

> Man does not feel that he is in danger. Good and evil no longer exist. Relativism, that terribly effective bleach, has wiped out everything in its path. Doctrinal and moral confusion is reaching its height. Evil is good, good is evil. Man no longer feels any need to be saved. The loss of the sense of salvation is the consequence of the loss of the transcendence of God.[328]

Enlightenment philosophy permeates our culture, extolling the inherent goodness of humanity and dismissing the need for reliance upon God or for faith. Human reason is sufficient. "Very few people consider themselves to be fallen creatures in need of a Savior."[329] However, with the evaporation of faith comes a corresponding increase in listlessness, despair, hopelessness, pessimism, boredom, and an ongoing search for purpose. "Anyone who is so 'progressive' as not to remain in the teaching of the Christ does not have God ..."[330] In short, without God, we cannot be who we were created to be,[331] and we are doomed to be restless wanderers, seeking purpose and meaning without finding it, and with no hope of achieving our true destiny: eternal blessedness in the life to come.

Pope Francis wrote, "The Joy of the Gospel fills the hearts and lives of all who encounter Jesus. Those who accept his offer of salvation are set free from sin, sorrow, inner emptiness and loneliness."[332] Accordingly, it all begins with the need for encounter that comes through silent contemplation and prayer. In light of this, consider the advice of St. Ignatius Brianchaninov" "The necessary, essential condition for progress in the Jesus Prayer is living according to the

---

328 Cardinal Robert Sarah, *The Day is Now Far Spent*, 47.
329 Brianchaninov, *The Refuge*, 307. Note that Brianchaninov died in 1867, yet this same issue persists to the present day.
330 2 John 9.
331 Humanity was created to live in union with God, to share in his eternal blessedness. Secular culture dismisses this purpose, which in turn, contributes to fruitless attempts to find meaning and purpose in life.
332 Pope Francis, *Evangelii Gaudium*, no. 1

commandments of the Lord Jesus."[333] We will come back to this later in the chapter.

The Need for Our Savior

Once a person understands and accepts the need for salvation, he or she begins to understand the need for the Savior. We cannot achieve salvation on our own. Rather, we must rely on Divine assistance (*synergeia*) to achieve our goal. Looking to the Gospels, the rich young man asked Jesus, "Teacher, what good must I do to gain eternal life?"[334] Jesus responded, "Why do you ask me about the good? There is only One who is good. If you wish to enter into life, keep the commandments."[335] The young man told Jesus that he kept all of these and asked, "What do I still lack?"[336] To this, Jesus answered: ".If you wish to be perfect go, sell what you have and give to the poor, and you will have treasure in heaven. Then come, follow me."[337]

We know how the story ends. The rich young man went away sad, "for he had many possessions."[338] There are several important factors to note about this incident. First, when the young man walked away, Jesus did not run after him and say, "Wait! If that is too hard, maybe we can relax the standards a bit." There was no compromise to the teachings of Jesus and we all have the freedom to accept or reject "the offer of salvation." To this, disciples became concerned and asked, "Who then can be saved?"[339] As Jesus said, and which is important for this discussion, "For human beings this is impossible, but for God all things are possible."[340] This comes back to the importance of *synergeia*, human-divine collaboration. We need to

---

333 Brianchaninov, *The Refuge*, 256.
334 Matt. 19:16.
335 Matt. 19:17.
336 Matt. 19:20.
337 Matt. 19:21.
338 Matt. 19:22.
339 Matt. 19:23.
340 Matt. 19:26.

freely surrender our will (self-will) to God, just as Jesus did, in order to achieve eternal life. Elsewhere, Jesus says, "Remain in me"[341] and "Without me you can do nothing."[342] We simply cannot do it on our own ("for human beings this impossible"). In short, we become increasingly more God-like (*theosis*) through the cooperation of free will and divine grace.[343]

In the Jesus Prayer, we acknowledged our reliance on God: *Lord Jesus Christ, Son of God, have mercy on me, a sinner*. We ask for the one item we most need: his mercy.

Jesus as the Way

Accepting Jesus as "the way"[344] to salvation, let us examine his teaching in more depth because it will give us a greater appreciation for the Art of Spiritual Life. Consider Jesus's statement, "If anyone wishes to come after me, he must deny himself and take up his cross daily and follow me."[345]

1. Self-Denial

St. Ignatius Brianchaninov suggested this self-denial consists of three labors: solitude, fasting, and vigil. It should be noted that in teachings of these Church Fathers, all Christians, lay and monastics alike, are called to holiness.[346]

---

341 John 15:4.

342 John 15:5.

343 See Archimandrite Aimilianos of Simonopetra, *The Church at Prayer*, ed. The Holy Convent of the Annunciation, Ormylia (Alhambra, CA: Sebastian Press, 2012), 44. Simonopetra is one of the major monasteries on Mount Athos.

344 See John 14:6. "I am the way and the truth and the life. No one comes to the Father except through me."

345 Luke 9:23.

346 See Brianchaninov, *The Refuge*, 298. "It is absolutely necessary for all Christians, lay or monastic, to fulfill the command of the Savior with all diligence: 'For whoever desires to save his life will lose it, but whoever loses his life for my sake and the gospel's will save it' (Mark 8:35)."

a. **Solitude**

This first labor relates to inner stillness, which includes withdrawal, stillness, and encountering Jesus in the silence of our hearts. "The true servant of God is invited into such solitude by the Holy Spirit himself."[347] In such silence, we are alone with God and listen to what he asks of us. Such solitude includes the interior silence of our minds as well as elimination of external distractions. Thus, it also includes the ascetical practices conducive to creating the environment of encounter, not being weighed down by material goods, and it means a withdrawal from the world, removing ourselves from ongoing temptation. We need to avoid places and people who will lead us away from Christ, as well as physically withdrawing for times of prayer (daily in our inner room, regularly on retreat, etc.), so that we can be alone, as Jesus was with his Father.

Preserve your mind. Keep life as simple as possible. What is necessary? What is sufficient? Consider the example of Mother Teresa and "her prescription." What do we need for our daily living in terms of housing, clothes, car, food, vacations? An American doctor who worked with Mother Teresa wrote:

> We surround ourselves with discontent and dissatisfaction because we believe that having something different or better will make our life better. Contentment, however, does not mean giving up a desire for more or a desire for something better. It simply means that today I will be happy with what happens to me. I will be content

---

347 Brianchaninov, *The Refuge*, 292.

with my life, knowing that I am doing the best I can, and that what follows is God's will. As Mother Teresa often said, "God does not make mistakes." By directing my life to its proper purpose and disciplining my mind to Mother's prescription for living, I can be content. I know that the consequences are as they should be since they are God's will. I can be content knowing that I thought, spoke, and acted well. [348]

Excessive or beautiful things immediately draw the heart's inclination to them, and then the mind will be distracted, and begin to wander.[349] We can often do with less than we think, far less. It is the spirit of the age that leads us a consumerist life that leads us away from the Gospel and disturbs our inner sense of stillness.

b. **Fasting**

The second labor is moderate fasting. St. Ignatius Brianchaninov wrote:

Fasting is the foundation of all monastic labors; without it, it is impossible to preserve solitude, to rein in the tongue, to lead a sober, attentive life, to succeed in prayer and vigil to acquire a remembrance of death, to see the multitude of one's own sins.[350]

---

348 See Paul A. Wright, MD, *Mother Teresa's Prescription: Finding Happiness and Peace in Service* (Notre Dame, IN: Ave Maria Press, 2006), 81.
349 See Brianchaninov, *The Refuge* , 293.
350 Ibid., 296.

From earliest times, the Church Fathers have said that an overindulgence in food enflames the other passions: lust, pride, greed, vanity, arrogance, among them. Most spiritual writers reference St. John Climacus's seminal work, *The Ladder of Divine Ascent*. He specifically addressed gluttony and says, "Control your appetites ... let us restrain our appetites with the thought of the fire to come."[351] Likewise, he wrote: "[T]he man who looks after his belly and at the same time hopes to control the spirit of [lust] is like someone trying to put out a fire with oil."[352] Desert Father Abba Pimen adds, "How can you perceive in yourself the fear of God when your stomach is filled with pies and cheeses?"[353] Such luxuries and temporal pleasures dull the senses, diminishing our need for God and salvation. As Cardinal Sarah wrote, "We do not believe we are in danger."

Fasting should be considered in terms of all passions. Generally, the two most common and challenging to control are pride (and its many related children: vanity, anger, impatient, arrogance, and gossiping, just to name a few) and lust.[354] Self-denial and self-control are essential components of following Jesus and are also an essential part of the Art of Spiritual Life. Accordingly, we are encouraged to have rigor around these disciplines, abstaining from certain foods, limiting the number of meals and quantities of food eaten at each meal, and avoiding food in between

---

351 St. John Climacus, *The Ladder of Divine Ascent*, 167. Step 14: On Gluttony. The literal translation of "appetites" references "the belly." For most ascetical writers, gluttony and lust are always closely connected.

352 Ibid., 168.

353 Abba Pimen (Poemen), *Apophthegmata Patrum*. Cited by Brianchaninov, *The Refuge*, 297.

354 See St. Theophan the Recluse, *The Path to Salvation: A Concise Outline of Christian Ascesis*, transl. Seraphim Rose (Stafford, AZ: St. Paisius Monastery), 47. He defined anger and lust as the "fiercest" of the passions. He reposed in 1894. Today, many priests say that anger and pornography are the two sins most often heard in the Sacrament of Confession, indicative of the tenacity of these passions.

meals. Curbing the tongue may include avoiding certain situations or people, anything that would cause us to judge or speak ill of others. Controlling lust may also mean avoiding certain temptations, locations, entertainment, or people who could cause the mind to wander.

Fasting is an essential labor required to follow Jesus and develop a deeper relationship with him. The problem in today's world is that we rarely hear about fasting, and the requirements seem quite minimalist. Therefore, we undertake greater struggles, realizing we cannot do it alone. Accordingly, we pray to Jesus for the help to draw our hearts closer to him, surrendering our desires and will to him. *Lord Jesus Christ, Son of God, have mercy on me, a sinner.* When we are being tempted or struggling, the Jesus Prayer is an excellent weapon with which to enter the battle.

c. **Vigil**

This third labor involves a number of activities, most notably, dedicating specific time to prayer, such as part of a Rule of Prayer. Herein, the person stands before the door of God's mercy during his time of solitary prayer.[355] This is when the Jesus Prayer is used, to align one's mind and heart with God. It is also a time to remember and mourn our sinfulness (*penthos*), how we've failed God and have fallen short of what he asks of us. In addition, it means maintaining a specific discipline concerning liturgical services.

d. **Summary of Labors**

These three labors generally are associated with ascetics. Through labors such as these, we learn self-denial

---

355 See Brianchaninov, *The Refuge*, 294.

in order to more closely follow Christ. The objective, of course, is to surrender our own will to the Divine will, which requires significant struggle—the battle never ending until our last breath.

2. Taking Up the Cross

"If anyone wishes to come after me, he must ... take up his cross daily ..." As St. Ignatius Brianchaninov wrote:

> To make a physical cross, you need two connected crossbars. To make a spiritual cross, you also need two spiritual crossbars. The first is sorrows undertaken willingly, that is, ascetic labors that crucify the flesh and keep it in such a state of crucifixion. The second is external sorrows that rein in and humble the spirit of man that is constantly inclined toward pride because of its damage by the Fall. The connection of these sorrows creates that cross that we are commanded to take up and with which we are to follow Christ. Without this cross, [imitation] of Christ is impossible.[356]

The first bar of our spiritual cross consists of voluntarily denying ourselves, stripping away our attachments.[357] Given the secular world in which we live, we are constantly bombarded by a media blitz as to all the things we need. Buying and consuming such things will make us happy. Yet as Pope Francis wrote:

---

356 Brianchaninov, *The Refuge*, 295.
357 A greater examination of this is undertaken in Kleinguetl, *Choosing Life in Christ*, 45-74. This is the Conference entitled "Formation" and discusses how we follow the example of Christ to form us as authentic disciples.

The great danger in today's world, pervaded as it is by consumerism, is the desolation and anguish born of a complacent yet covetous heart, the feverish pursuit of frivolous pleasures, and a blunted conscience. Whenever our interior life becomes caught up in our own interests and concerns, there is no longer room for others, no place for the poor. God's voice is no longer heard, the quiet joy of his love is no longer felt, and the desire to do good fades. This is a very real danger for believers too. Many fall prey to it, and end up resentful, angry, and listless. That is no way to live a dignified and fulfilled life; it is not God's will for us, nor is it the life in the Spirit which has its source in the heart of the Risen Christ.[358]

Accordingly, we discipline ourselves through self-denial to desire less and have a right-ordered relationship with our possessions. Recall the conversation on the Mother Teresa's "prescription": What is necessary and what is extraneous?

In terms of the second bar, these are generally struggles that come our way through the ordinary circumstances of life: sickness, death, adversity, insults, financial failings, persecution. In many cases, instead of us voluntarily seeking the desert, the desert finds us instead.

So, why are we tested? This seems to be the antithesis of the prevailing culture, which in many corners, implies that if one lives virtuously, he or she should be spared suffering.[359] However, Jesus is clear. His way is the Way of the Cross, which

---

358 Pope Francis, *Evangelii Gaudium*, no. 2.
359 This was also a prevailing belief of the Pharisees at the time of Jesus.

means that suffering is generally part of the package. It is through suffering that we begin to understand our true humanity, our fallen nature, and our sinfulness. Once we see the depths to which we have fallen, we begin to more clearly recognize our need for God. Without suffering, without the cross, we will not truly know our need for salvation, our true distance from God, or to recognize and accept our Savior as we should.[360]

How often do we fall into sin, give into temptation, or become overwhelmed by our circumstances? How often do go along with the crowd, justifying an action as right based on popular opinion instead of the teachings of the Gospel? If we are honest with ourselves, we are weak and give in easily. The only way to overcome our passions and the demons that torment us is through Jesus.

Lord Jesus Christ, Son of God, have mercy on me, a sinner.

It is through our trials that we learn to surrender, to empty ourselves of self, and allow the Holy Spirit to fill us. Like children, we are proud and stubborn, wanting to do things ourselves. We resist help and think our plan is better than God's (a classic illusion). However, only through the act of surrender will we generally find peace and a path forward.

Jesus told his disciples, "For whoever wishes to save his life will lose it, but whoever loses his life for my sake and that of the gospel will save it."[361] Consider this more carefully. What life are we trying to save? This is the life offered to us by the secular world with all its promises of happiness and fulfillment influenced by the spirit of the age. It is a world in which we do not need God; we can indulge our passions without restraint. Eat, drink, and be merry. We try

360 See Brianchaninov, *The Refuge*, 314.
361 Mark 8:35.

to "save" this life because we live in this world and often find ourselves deeply attracted to this world. However, we will lose this life because it leads to sin, sorrow, inner emptiness, and loneliness. Further, because of sin, we will also lose our eternal life, having chosen to separate ourselves from God and his offer of salvation. This is *not* the abundant life God wants for us.[362] "The gate is wide and the road broad that leads to destruction, and those who enter through it are many."[363] We have to understand upfront, the way of Jesus will be the road less traveled and will often stand in stark contradiction to the "norms" of our world.

Looking at the reverse, if we lose our lives in the secular world, we will gain true life. Only the teaching of the Gospel leads us to true life and, to gain this life, we must follow the example of Jesus, who is the way.[364] "How narrow the gate and constricted the road that leads to life. And those who find it are few."[365] Sadly, few will make the choice to stay the course and follow Jesus.

To recognize our true fallen nature, how truly far we are from God, is scary. We do not want to acknowledge it, desiring instead to delude ourselves: "It is not really all that bad ..." We find ourselves in a dark abyss created by our sinfulness, desperately trying to find our way back to the Father. By feeling the acute pain of our separation, we can begin to mourn our sinfulness (compunction) and we will begin to realize Jesus is our Redeemer and Savior and how much we need him. It is then we can cry out with true humility, *Lord Jesus Christ, Son of God, have mercy on me, a sinner.*

---

362 See John 10:10.
363 Matt. 7:13.
364 See John 14:6.
365 Matt. 7:14.

Let us examine the idea of our separation from God in further depth.

a. The Grace to Understand Our Fallen Nature

Our objective is to be honest with ourselves. We can only do this with grace granted by God (*synergeia*). So we pray for this grace: O Lord, grant me the grace to see myself as you see me—not as I see myself or as others see me. Allow me:

- To see my sinfulness, brokenness, and need for mercy.

- To see that the very salvation of my soul is at risk.

- To truly mourn my sinfulness and fallen nature with many tears.

- To recognize how far my heart has wandered from you, Lord.

- To recognize, like the Prodigal, my desire to leave the pigpen and come home to you—to feel your warm embrace of divine love and to hear those words, "My child has returned from the dead."[366]

My Lord, I am nothing without you. *Lord Jesus Christ, Son of God, have mercy on me, a sinner.*

b. The Risk of Delusion

In a homily, Archimandrite Aimilianos of Simonopetra said:

> What an inaccessible place it is! We know everything. But we have no idea what's contained in our own heart—what

---

366 See the Parable of the Prodigal Son, Luke 15:11-32.

> a morass, what passions, what rottenness, what darkness—that we do not know. Each of us thinks he's a personality, that he is a saint! That he's "somebody" who can stand before God and say to him: "My God, my God, I've given you this, I've devoted myself to you, I've done this, that, and the other thing for you …"[367]

Our self-perception can be delusional. Without knowing our true spiritual condition, without knowing the depths of our fallen nature, without recognizing our true sinfulness or our actual separation from God, it is easy to become deceived into complacency, thinking our efforts are "good enough." We justify our lives (e.g., "we're doing better than most"), steering away from or trying to widen the narrow path or seeking an easier middle path (of which there is none). All this "is a clear sign of spiritual disorder and a deviation from the path to salvation."[368] If we do not have a true understanding of our fallen nature, we may dismiss our need for salvation and be haphazard in cultivating a relationship with our Savior. This leads, at best, to a lukewarm faith, spiritual atrophy, and ultimately to spiritual death. As one writer said, "Living on the surface of life leads us to a toxic self-interest."[369] This self-interest will always preclude us from a relationship with the Divine.

c. Knowing Our True Selves

To come to know our true selves, we take up our

---

367 Archimandrite Aimilianos, *The Church at Prayer*, 23.
368 Brianchaninov, *The Refuge*, 299.
369 Cf. David G.R. Keller, *Oasis of Wisdom: The Worlds of the Desert Fathers and Mothers* (Collegeville, MN: Liturgical Press, 2005), 3.

crosses daily, both those we voluntarily endure in terms of self-denial and detachment (ascetical practices), and those given to us by God to bear when we ask, "Give us this day our daily bread."[370]

As Dorotheos of Gaza (c. 505-565) wrote:

> Above all let us be convinced that nothing can happen to us apart from the providence of God.[371]

He adds:

> In God's providence everything is absolutely right and whatever happens is for the assistance of the soul. For whatever God does with us, he does out of love and consideration for us because it is adapted to our needs.[372]

God invites us through such challenges to surrender and allow him to guide us through the situation.[373] It is through our struggles wherein God recognizes our true desire for him and we begin to realize our spiritual potential.[374]

---

370 Most pray this daily in the Lord's Prayer (Our Father), and yet do we know what we are truly asking of God? We essentially tell God that he knows what we need and he should provide it for us. Sometimes, there is a great divide between what we think we need and what God thinks we need. Surrendering to the will of God means we will be content with whatever he chooses to give us, a blessing or a significant challenge. See also Jer. 29:11-14. Also, in some respects, the Lord's Prayer is the perfect complement to the Jesus Prayer. In the Prayer, we ask for the one thing we need from God, mercy, because the Father already knows what we need before we ask (see Matt. 6:8). In the Lord's Prayer, we ask for "our daily bread"—everything else that God believes we need, leaving it up to him.

371 Dorotheos of Gaza, *Discourses and Sayings*, transl. Eric P. Wheeler (Kalamazoo, MI: Cistercian Publications, 1977), 143. Discourse VII, "On Self-accusation."

372 Ibid., 192. Discourse XIII, "On Enduring Temptation Calmly and Thankfully."

373 Consider the Surrender Novena of Fr. Dolindo Ruotolo (1882-1970): "O Jesus, I surrender myself to you, take care of everything!"

374 Archimandrite Aimilianos, *The Church at Prayer*, 16 and 18.

Archimandrite Aimilianos advised us that God expects us to work at this relationship:

> First, so that will express our longing for him, and for that longing to be uniquely ours (i.e., a free-will choice). Second, so that we can become aware of our need and nakedness, and third, so that we can learn to seek him."[375]

Without the struggle and incremental progress, "We'd cast him (God) aside as easily as we'd won him, because would not have understood the true value."[376]

As written in the Second Letter of Peter:

> Therefore, brothers, be all the more eager to make your call and election firm, for, in doing so, you will never stumble. For, in this way, entry into the eternal kingdom of our Lord and savior Jesus Christ will be richly provided for you.[377]

d. The Way of the Cross

The crosses we are given are part of God's wisdom and plan for our salvation. We are tested so our commitment to follow Jesus is unshakable. As St. Paul wrote, "affliction produces endurance, and endurance, proven character, and proven character, hope, and hope does not disappoint..."[378] Jesus tells us he is the way to the Father and that way is through the cross.

---

375 Ibid., 18.
376 Ibid.
377 2 Pet. 1:10-11.
378 Rom. 5:4-5.

3. Following Jesus

"If anyone wishes to come after me, he must ... follow me." What does it mean to "follow Christ" after denying ourselves and taking up our crosses? "To follow Jesus means to live our earthly lives only for heaven, just as Jesus lived his own life.[379] We are called to live the God-like virtues of humility, obedience, and patient endurance in imitation of Jesus. When this seems impossible, we need to reflect on who Jesus is, the God-man, truly human and truly divine. He is our guide to the Father and he is our end goal, divinized humanity, living in union with God.[380] Jesus tells us that apart from him, we can do nothing.[381] So, it is clear we need Divine assistance for the journey (*synergeia*), which more often than not, may seem to us like Peter walking on the water[382] and crying out in fear, "Lord, save me!"[383] (*Lord Jesus Christ, Son of God, have mercy on me, a sinner.*) Our singular focus must be heaven and we should live our lives accordingly. As Jesus told his disciples, "Seek first the kingdom of God and his righteousness ..."[384] We are not to worry about anything else because the Father knows what we need and he will provide it.[385]

By following Jesus, by truly coming to know him and making him a companion on our journey to eternal blessedness, we will find warmth of heart, joy, and peace—even in the midst of adversity. Recall the encounter of the two disciples on the road to Emmaus ("Were not our hearts burning within us"[386]). As St. Theophan the Recluse wrote, "A true witness of Christian life is

---

379 Brianchaninov, *The Refuge*, 296.
380 See Edward Kleinguetl, *Choosing Life in Christ: A Vocation to Holiness* (Parker, CO: Outskirts Press, 2019), 102-104. This includes a discussion on "Who is Jesus Christ?"
381 Cf. John 15:5.
382 See Matt. 14:22-33.
383 Matt. 14:30.
384 Matt. 6:33.
385 See Matt. 6:25-34. Jesus describes placing complete dependence on God.
386 Luke 24:32.

the fire of active zeal for the pleasing of God."[387] Consider the examples of Mother Teresa, Dorothy Day, Fr. Walter Ciszek, St. Elizabeth of the Trinity, St. Anna Schäffer, Blessed Pier Giorgio Frassati, Blessed Theodore Romzha, Blessed Emilian Kovch, or Cardinal Francis Xavier Nguyen Van Thuan.[388] All had a zeal for serving God in variety of circumstances, many involving tremendous struggles or suffering.

What ignites the spark? What produces the zeal? It begins with coming to experience the Risen Jesus in silent contemplation and prayer. This is the foundation. When we come to truly know Jesus and desire him above all else, we will find the divine life roused in our hearts through the working of the Holy Spirit. This creates the fire.

Summarizing the Art of Spiritual Life

The Art of Spiritual Life is about establishing a rhythm in daily living that fosters a deeper interior life, living in true relationship with Jesus. It is about interior disposition, cultivating the soil of our hearts so that the seeds planted therein will produce a fruitful harvest. Some also refer to this as interior monasticism, rediscovering how everyday laypeople, also called to holiness, can benefit from spiritual practices taken from the monks. Through this process of cultivating our hearts, we become increasingly aware of our longing and need for God, recognizing his presence in our daily activities and struggles, and surrendering our self-will to God's will. Through these efforts, we increasingly collaborate with God's plan for our lives (*synergeia*) in order to draw closer to him, to experience joy and fulfillment, and prepare ourselves for our destiny: union with God in the life to

---

387 St. Theophan the Recluse, *The Path to Salvation*, 27.
388 See Edward Kleinguetl, *Into the Desert: The Wisdom of the Desert Fathers and Mothers* (Parker, CO: Outskirts Press, 2019), 80-86. This includes examples from the modern "cloud of witnesses" (Heb. 12:1), with examples of how people followed Jesus through fervency of faith and some through great chastisements.

come. In many cases, the Art of Spiritual Life is really about getting back to the basics of our faith: prayer, fasting, almsgiving, increased participation in the sacramental life of the Church (especially the Holy Mysteries of Repentance and Holy Eucharist), ongoing study of Sacred Scripture particularly the Gospels for guidance, and reading from the writings of the Spiritual Fathers and Mothers who have gone before us and how they handled the same struggles we face today. We do not need a new plan of action. Plans already exist, along with much spiritual wisdom to guide us along the way.

Prayer—particularly the Jesus Prayer—is an essential foundational component of the spiritual life, whereby we come to know the Risen Jesus in the depth of our hearts, learn to increasingly rely on him, ultimately becoming completely dependent upon him, and allowing him to lead us to the Father in Heaven. We cannot achieve our salvation without him because we are too weak and steeped in our sinful nature. The Jesus Prayer is one of the critical weapons that allow us to undertake the struggles we will encounter along the way, and the more we live a Christ-centered life, the more this creates an environment conducive to prayer and ongoing formation.

While we have placed a focus on prayer in this work, the reality is that it is difficult to extricate prayer from the other components of the spiritual life. These components are indelibly linked. Herein, we can think back to the Simple Path of Mother Teresa:

> The fruit of silence is prayer.
> The fruit of prayer is faith.
> The fruit of faith is love.
> The fruit of love is service.
> The fruit of service is peace.

Therein, we can envision how love of God is deepened through authentic encounter achieved in silent contemplation and prayer. This, in turn, strengthens our faith, creating a fire within and drawing us to love God, which, in turn, manifests itself in love of neighbor. In the end, we begin to experience in our hearts the peace the world cannot give; only Jesus himself can give us inner peace.[389] This spiritual journey and our related growth in faith is highly interdependent, rooted in silence, the fruit of which is prayer.

If we acquire divine grace, all things are easy, joyful, and a blessing from God. Come now and find me a religion that makes man perfect and happy! And what a pity we don't comprehend this extraordinary quality in our religion! [390]

—Elder Porphyrios of Kavsokalyvia

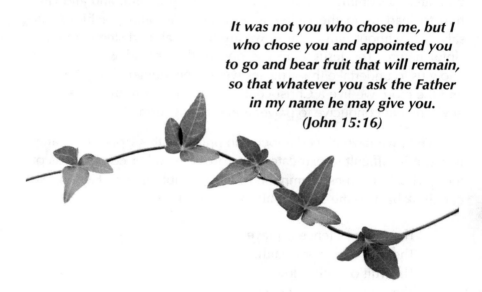

It was not you who chose me, but I who chose you and appointed you to go and bear fruit that will remain, so that whatever you ask the Father in my name he may give you.
(John 15:16)

---

389 See John 14:27. "Peace I leave with you; my peace I give to you. Not as the world gives do I give it to you. Do not let your hearts be troubled or afraid."
390 Elder Porphyrios, *Wounded by Love*, 131.

Some Final Reflections for the Journey

"My sacrifice, O God, is a contrite spirit; a contrite,
humbled heart, O God, you will not scorn."
(Psalm 51:19)

Dear Fellow Pilgrim,

In this book, we have focused on prayer as a means of establishing a relationship with the Divine Presence that dwells in every human heart and how it is a foundational skill to The Art of Spiritual Life. As we conclude this particular work, we want to leave you with some reflections from the Tradition to reinforce our discussion herein. These are just a few proofs of how we are heirs to a faith that is ever ancient, ever new, a Deposit of Faith that can be traced back to Jesus and his Apostles. May we be inspired and take courage that we are following the right path to eternal blessedness and not succumb to the distortions that are prevalent in the prevailing culture of our day.

On Prayer

Opening Gospel Reading

Read: Matt. 6:1-8 (Teachings on Almsgiving and Prayer).

St. John Chrysostom (c.349 – 407)

As background, John was born in Antioch and as part of Christian life, he spent two years (c. 375-377) living in extreme asceticism in the wilderness as a hermit, fasting, praying, and memorizing Sacred Scriptures. Afterward, he returned to Antioch where he was tonsured a reader, later ordained a deacon, and then a priest (386). In 397, he was appointed Archbishop of Constantinople. During his time in ordained ministry, he wrote a significant number of homilies, many of which have been preserved. The following reflection is taken from one of these homilies and the reader will notice his reference to the ancient prayer practices we have been discussing, namely that which evolved and came to be known as the Jesus Prayer or the Prayer of the Heart.

Prayer is the Light of the Spirit

Prayer and converse with God is a supreme good: it is a partnership and union with God. As the eyes of the body are enlightened when they see light, so our spirit, when it is intent on God, is illuminated by his infinite light. I do not mean the prayer of outward observance, but prayer from the heart, not confined to fixed times or periods, but continuous throughout the day and night.

Our spirit should be quick to reach out toward God, not only when it is engaged in meditation; at other times also, when it is carrying out its duties, caring for the needy, performing works of charity, giving generously in the service of others, our spirit should long for God and call him to mind, so that these works may be seasoned with the salt of God's love, and so make a palatable offering to the Lord of the universe. Throughout the whole of our lives, we may enjoy the benefit that comes from prayer if we devote a great deal of time to it.

Prayer is the light of the spirit, true knowledge of God, mediating between God and man. The spirit, raised up to heaven by prayer, clings to God with the utmost tenderness; like a child crying tearfully for its mother, it craves the milk

God provides. It seeks the satisfaction of its own desires, and receives gifts outweighing the whole world of nature.

Prayer stands before God as an honored ambassador. It gives joy to the spirit, peace to the heart. I speak of prayer, not words. It is the longing for God, love too deep for words, a gift not given by man, but by God's grace. The apostle Paul says: "We do not know how we are to pray but the Spirit himself pleads for us with in inexpressible longings" (Rom. 8:26).

When the Lord gives this type of prayer to a man, he gives him riches that cannot be taken away, heavenly food that satisfies the spirit. One who tastes this food is set on fire with an eternal longing for the Lord: his spirit burns as in a fire of the utmost intensity.

Practice prayer from the beginning. Paint your house with the colors of modesty and humility. Make it radiant with the light of justice. Decorate it with the finest gold leaf of good deeds. Adorn it with the walls and stones of faith and generosity. Crown it with the pinnacle of prayer. In this way, you will make it a perfect dwelling place for the Lord. You will be able to receive him as in a splendid palace, and through his grace you will already possess him, his image enthroned in the temple of the spirit.[391]

St. John Chrysostom is one of the early Doctors of the Church, a bishop whose pastoral teachings are deeply rooted in an experience of God in prayer. In this brief reflection, we observe a number of the themes that have been previously discussed: a prayer which is beyond words, prayer from the heart, a gift given by God, to be practiced from the beginning and to devote a great deal of time to it, that it continues unceasingly throughout the day and night, enhances our good works, unites us with God, and creates a "splendid palace"

---

391 St. John Chrysostom, *De Precatione*, Homily 6. Taken from *The Liturgy of the Hours*, vol. 2. New York: The Catholic Book Publishing Company, 1976. 68-70.

into which to welcome the Divine Presence (the kingdom of God within you—Luke 17:21). He wrote, "Prayer is the light of the spirit," which is a similar perspective to St. Seraphim of Sarov, who said that the objective of prayer is the acquisition of the Holy Spirit. One of the concepts discussed herein is warmth of the heart, to which Chrysostom notes that the one who has prayer "is set on fire with an eternal longing for the Lord: his spirit burns as in a fire of the utmost intensity." Thus, prayer creates the shining, inextinguishable light that bears witness to the world in which we live. At the beginning in the Introduction, we said that if we want to be radical, if want to reform the Church and our world, learn prayer. Finally, when considering this reflection in the context of our prior discussions herein, we can recognize an unbroken thread of a prayer tradition that emerged, and was practiced and preserved from the very Early Church to today.

On Fasting

Opening Gospel Reading

Read: Matt. 6:16-18 (Teaching on Fasting).

Creating the Environment for Prayer

We have previously discussed the fact that prayer cannot be isolated from The Art of Spiritual Life. We must create the correct environment to nurture prayer and our relationship with God, which includes ascetical practices such as fasting and self-denial. Thus, our next reflection revolves around this theme.

St. Symeon the New Theologian (949-1022)

At an early age, Symeon was convinced by a well-known monk to give his own life to prayer and asceticism. By the time he was thirty, he became the abbot of the Monastery of St. Mammas near Constantinople, a position he held for nearly 25 years. He was one of the first of the Byzantine mystics to freely share his spiritual experiences for the benefit of others and also stressed the importance of having a spiritual father. Because of his insights to the spiritual life, he is one of three saints within the Eastern Churches given the title of "theologian," the other two being St. John the Apostle and Evangelist, and St. Gregory of Nazianzus (329-390).[392] The reflection is taken from his work, *The Discourses*, which was a series of homilies and teachings shared with his fellow monks at the Monastery of St. Mammas. In context, this teaching was given at the end of the first week of Lent (the Great Fast).

Holy Fasting

> Let each one of us keep in mind the benefit of fasting and what gifts from God he has enjoyed in these few days and so become more eager for the days to come. For this healer of our souls is effective, in the case of one to quieten the fevers and impulses of the flesh, in another to assuage bad temper, in yet another to drive away sleep, in another to stir up zeal, and in yet another to restore purity of mind and to set him free from evil thoughts. In one it will control his unbridled tongue and ... restrain it by the fear of God and prevent it from uttering idle or corrupt words (Eph. 4:29; Matt. 12:36). In another it will visibly guard his eyes and fix them on high instead of allowing them to roam hither and thither, and thus cause him to look on himself and teach him to be mindful of his own faults and shortcomings.

> Fasting gradually disperses and drives away spiritual darkness and the veil of sin that lies on the soul, just as the sun dispels the mist. Fasting enables us spiritually to see that spiritual air in which Christ, the Sun who knows no setting, does not rise,

---

392 In the Eastern Christian Tradition, *theologia (θεολογία)* means a relationship with God that transcends knowledge, and a theologian is one who has a direct experience of God. There is a well-known and often quoted axiom in Eastern Christian spirituality taken from the writings of Evagrius Ponticus: "If you are a theologian you truly pray. If you truly pray you are a theologian."

but shines without ceasing. Fasting, aided by vigil, penetrates and softens hardness of heart ... I beseech you, let each of us strive that this may happen to us!

It is not possible for these things to come about in one day or one week! This will take much time, labor, and pain, in accordance with each man's attitude and willingness, according to the measure of faith (Rom. 12:3, 6) and one's contempt for the objectives of sight and thought. In addition, it is also in accordance with the fervor of his ceaseless penitence and its constant working in the secret chamber of his heart (Matt. 6:6) that this is accomplished more quickly or more slowly by the gift and grace of God. But without fasting, no one was ever able to achieve any of these virtues or any others, for fasting is the beginning and foundation of every spiritual activity. Whatever you will build on this foundation cannot collapse or be destroyed, because they are built on solid rock Matt. 7:24-25). But if you remove this foundation and substitute for it a full stomach and improper desires, they will be undermined like sand by evil thoughts, and the whole structure of virtues will be destroyed (cf. Matt. 7:26; Luke 6:49).

To prevent this from happening in our case ... let us gladly stand on the solid foundation of fasting. Let us stand firmly, let us stand willingly![393]

In Chapter 5, we discussed The Art of Spiritual Life and the importance of fasting and ascetical practices as part of the spiritual journey in conjunction with prayer. The focus of such practices is placed on surrender of self-will to the Divine will, allowing for divine-human collaboration (*synergeia*) required for individual transformation (*theosis*), preparing us for eternal blessedness in the life to come. Jesus himself instructed us that those who wish

---

393 St. Symeon the New Theologian, "Holy Fasting," Magnificat 21, no. 12 (February 2020): 405-406. Taken from *The Discourses* Translated by C.J. de Catanzaro. New York: The Paulist Press, 1980. 167-169.

to come after him, to follow him to the abundant life promised by God, must deny themselves, take up their crosses daily, and follow him.[394] Accordingly, this reflection is from a spiritual master from the Jesus Prayer tradition. It discusses the importance of fasting and its impact on personal purification, giving us the ability to overcome the passions and temptations that assail us. St. Symeon references key thoughts such as this "effective healer of souls" and also refers to the fear of God, which is the foundation for all virtue. This complements what St. Isaac the Syrian wrote, "There can be no knowledge of God on a full stomach,"[395] and St. Ignatius Brianchaninov's instruction with regard to the Jesus Prayer, "Start with a stomach that is not too full."[396]

On Almsgiving

Opening Gospel Reading

Read: Matt. 6:1-4 (Teaching about Almsgiving).

Responding to Our Relationship with God

Through prayer, our love for God increases as our relationship with him deepens. Our heart is set on fire as a result of our encounters, creating a greater capacity to love others. Jesus was clear in his teaching when asked about the greatest commandment: "The second is like it: You shall love your neighbor as yourself."[397] In terms of the definition of "neighbor," Christ also made it clear in the Parable of the Good Samaritan that this term applies to anyone in need.[398] This significantly broadened the definition of neighbor from that to which the people at the time were accustomed. They avoided pagans and tax collectors (and especially Samaritans!), yet the interaction between the Samaritan of the parable and the man who fell victim to

---

394 Cf. Luke 9:23.
395 *The Ascetical Homilies of Saint Isaac the Syrian*, 146. Homily Four.
396 Brianchaninov, *The Refuge*, 134.
397 Matt. 22:39.
398 See Luke 10:25-37.

robbers shattered this taboo. In essence, since we are all made in the divine image, we are all neighbors to each another.

Almsgiving is the third of the penitential practices and is defined in the Catechism of the Catholic Church as "a witness to fraternal charity" and "a work of justice pleasing to God."[399] More than simply giving money or works of philanthropy, it involves a conversion of heart, being moved to compassion as Jesus was in response to the poor, the sick, the suffering, and the marginalized. Almsgiving is essentially an extension of our prayer because love of God manifests itself in love of neighbor.[400] Whoever is close to God is also close to his or her fellow human beings, images of God.

As a reflection, we once again consider a homily by St. John Chrysostom, who was well known for his teachings on wealth and poverty.

Love Christ as He Wishes to be Loved

> Do you want to honor Christ's body? Then do not scorn him in his nakedness, nor honor him here in the church with silken garments while neglecting him outside where he is cold and naked. For he who said, "This is my body," and made it so by his words, also said: "You saw me hungry and did not feed me," and "inasmuch as you did not do it for one of these, the least of my brothers, you did not do it for me." What we do here in the church requires a pure heart, not special garments; what we do outside requires great dedication.

> Let us learn, therefore, to be men of wisdom and to honor Christ as he desires. For a person being honored finds greatest pleasure in the honor he desires, not the honor we think best. Peter thought he was honoring Christ when he refused to let him wash his feet; but what Peter wanted was not truly an

---

399 *Catechism of the Catholic Church*, no. 2462.
400 See John 4:20. "If anyone says, 'I love God,' but hates his brother, he is a liar; for whoever does not love a brother whom he has seen cannot love God whom he has not seen."

honor, *quite the opposite!* Give him the honor prescribed in his law by giving your riches to the poor. For God does not want golden vessels, but golden hearts.

Now, in saying this I am not forbidding you to make such gifts; I am only demanding that along with such gifts and before them you give alms. He accepts the former, but he is much more pleased with the latter. In the former, only the giver profits; in the latter, the recipient does too. A gift to the church may be taken as a form of ostentation, but an alms is pure kindness.

Of what use is it to weigh down Christ's table with golden cups, when he himself is dying of hunger? First, fill him when he is hungry; then use the means you have left to adorn his table. Will you have a golden cup made but not give a cup of water? What is the use of providing the table with cloths woven of gold thread, and not providing Christ himself with the clothes he needs? What profit is there in that? Tell me: If you were to see him lacking the necessary food but were to leave him in that state and merely surround his table with gold, would he be grateful to you or rather would he not be angry? What if you were to see him clad in worn-out rags and stiff from cold, and were to forget about clothing him and instead were to set up gold columns for him, saying that you were doing it in his honor? Would he not think he was being mocked and greatly insulted?

Apply this also to Christ when he comes along the roads as a pilgrim, looking for shelter. You do not take him in as your guest, but you decorate the floor and walls and the capitals of the pillars. You provide silver chains for the lamps, but you cannot bear even to look at him as he lies chained in prison. Once again, I am not forbidding you to supply these adornments; I am urging you to provide these other things as well, and indeed to provide them first. No one has ever been accused for not providing ornaments, but for those who neglect their neighbor a hell waits with an inextinguishable fire and torment in the company of the demons. Do not, therefore, adorn the church and ignore your afflicted brother, *for he is the most precious temple of all.*[401]

Chrysostom reminds us that our love for God is manifested in love for neighbor, following the teachings and examples given by Jesus. For example, the above homily considers the teachings of Jesus on the Judgment of Nations,[402] which indicates that we will be judged worthy of entering the kingdom of heaven by how we loved the least among us. Returning to the Simple Path of St. Teresa of Calcutta:

> The fruit of silence is prayer.
> The fruit of prayer is faith.
> The fruit of faith is love.
> The fruit of love is service.
> The fruit of service is peace.

Accordingly, the relationship created with Jesus through prayer should increase our compassion for others. In terms of the three penitential practices, they complement each other, forming a foundation for our faith, and cannot be separated. As St. Peter Chrysologus (c.380-433) wrote: "Fasting is the soul of prayer, mercy is the lifeblood of fasting. Fasting bears no fruit unless it is watered by mercy."[403] Said yet another way, love of God should manifest itself in love of neighbor. Thus, we rightly ask ourselves: Through our encounters with the Divine Presence, how are we transformed? Do we begin to exhibit the God-like virtues of love, mercy, and compassion? From love flows forth service, the fruit of which is peace, an inner peace the world cannot give.[404]

---

401 St. John Chrysostom, "Gospel of Matthew," Homily 50. Taken from *The Liturgy of the Hours*, vol. IV (New York: Catholic Book Publishing Company, 1975), 182–183. Emphasis added by the author.
402 See Matt. 25:31-46.
403 St. Peter Chrysologus, "Sermon 43." Taken from *The Liturgy of the Hours*, vol. II (New York: Catholic Book Publishing Company, 1976), 231-232.
404 See John 14:27.

Conclusion

Our objective with these three brief reflections is to reinforce that the concepts we have discussed herein are not something new. There is no need for a new plan or strategy to fulfill human longing, to stand as a shining light to the darkness of the secular age, or obtain eternal blessedness and salvation. Jesus is the way, he showed us the way, and the Christian Tradition has faithfully preserved and continued on this narrow way since ancient times. The Art of Spiritual Life is a means for rediscovering this road with the guidance of the Holy Fathers who have traveled before us and are part of this rich Tradition.

The entire purpose of this work is to stress the importance of a spiritual life that possesses prayer at its foundation. If there is one wish we could have for our readers, it is to discover and possess the gift of prayer and to understand how this is such a critical component of discerning our true purpose in life: eternal blessedness with God. Prayer brings us into a deeper relationship with Jesus Christ, who is our ever-present, never-failing guide. St. Paisios of Mount Athos tells us:

> It is only near Christ that one can find actual, genuine joy, because only Christ gives actual joy and consolation. Wherever Christ is present, that is where true joy and the delight of Paradise are present. Those who are far from Christ do not have true joy.[405]

This is a message people today need to hear. In a world where the spirit of the age tries to distance itself from the Gospel of Jesus Christ and where people are frantically searching for meaning and purpose, this wisdom, this God-given gift of prayer, is what people need to discover or re-discover. Any other means of finding fulfillment is temporary at best and often leaves us empty. God alone will provide depth and meaning to our lives because humanity's entire purpose in life is to find him and make our way forward to the abundant life he offers us.

---

405 St. Paisios of Mount Athos, *Passions and Virtues*. Taken from "Spiritual Counsels," vol. V, transl. by Peter Chamberas, ed. Anna Famellos and Eleftheria Kaimakliotis (Souroti, Thessaloniki, Greece: Holy Monastery of Evangelist John the Theologian, 2016), 301.

Of course, prayer cannot be separated from the sacramental life of the Church because, together, they represent the fullness of the interior life. We chose to focus on prayer because many today have not been exposed or as fully formed with regard to this component of the spiritual life as compared to the Holy Mysteries. Further, as illustrated in the reflections above, prayer cannot be separated from fasting and almsgiving. The former helps create an environment conducive to prayer and the latter is a response to a deepened relationship with God. Thus, our objective is to help our readers and fellow pilgrims to develop a more rounded interior life with true prayer at its core.

For our part in this age, we are called to preserve this Deposit of Faith that has been entrusted to us by those who have gone before us, bearing witness to the world as to the true meaning of life, that which alone can provide us with inner peace and happiness. As Elder Porphyrios counseled, "We mustn't compromise the magnificence of our faith. We need to remain the people that we are and proclaim the truth and the light."[406] We are also called to accompany others on our united journey to seek eternal blessedness in the life to come.

May the Lord direct our steps
according to his holy will.

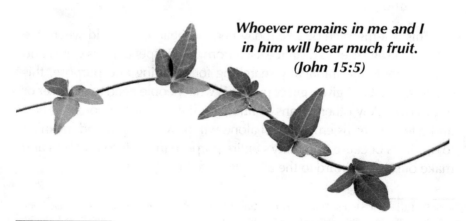

Whoever remains in me and I
in him will bear much fruit.
(John 15:5)

---

406 Elder Porphyrios, *Wounded by Love*, 211.

Glossary of Selected Terms

The following are selected terms related to our discussions herein and the concept of prayer and spirituality in general.

Acedia (ἀκηδία)   From the Greek meaning "negligence." *Acedia* is a gloomy combination of weariness, sadness, and a lack of purposefulness. It robs a person of the capacity for joy and leaves one feeling empty, or void of meaning. In the spiritual life, this equates to a state of listlessness or despondency, making it difficult to continue spiritual practices such as fasting, falling asleep during prayer or reading, and general boredom. Some Holy Fathers have considered this the most crushing of demons because it can cause a person to give up on the struggles associated with the spiritual journey. In a modern context, one would equate this with a person who is demoralized, or suffering from depression or burnout. The constant bombardment of Gospel values by secular society can exacerbate this condition.

Active Prayer   See "Self-Activating Prayer."

Agapé (ἀγάπη)   Greek term for the highest form of love. See "love."

Agnosticism   Rejection in belief defaulting to the view that matters of God are unknown or unknowable. God may exist but is not relevant. This is a popular perspective in today's society.

Almsgiving A penitential practice, sacrificially giving to God through charitable acts, assisting others in need. It is more than giving money or philanthropy. Rather, it is a conversion of heart, moved to compassion as Jesus was, and giving from our means, not just our surplus (see the widow's contribution, Luke 21:1-4). Almsgiving also becomes part of our prayer practice. Love of neighbor is an outflow from our love of God.

Apophatic An experience of God that transcends the possibility of being defined in words. Theologian Karl Rahner, SJ called this "themelessness"— we cannot capture God in words, concepts, or themes. We can only say something about God through our experiences, such as inferring his love for us. This theological perspective underpins the approach in Eastern Christian theology.

Apostolic Period The time of the Earliest Church, from the Ascension of Jesus to the death of the last apostle (ca. 100).

Art of Spiritual Life Establishing a rhythm in daily living that includes key spiritual practices such as prayer, fasting, and almsgiving. See also "Interior Monasticism." Includes regular study of the ascetical practices of the Fathers of the Church. The objectives are increasing awareness of our interior longing for God, ability to recognize his presence in our daily activities, and a focus on surrender of self-will to God's will. Through these efforts, we increasingly collaborate with God's plan for our lives (see *synergeia*) in order to draw closer to him, to experience joy and fulfillment, and prepare ourselves for our destiny: union with God in the life to come.

Asceticism

From the Greek *áskēsis* (ἄσκησις), meaning "exercise" or "training," similar to that done by an athlete. Asceticism as a spiritual discipline has three basic goals: (1) bringing order and self-control to human passions/appetites, (2) centering a person, and (3) opening a person to God's presence. Ascetical disciplines were meant as voluntary self-denial as prescribed by Jesus in his terms and conditions of discipleship ("If anyone wishes to come after me, he must *deny* himself and take up his cross daily and follow me" – Luke 9:23).

Atheism

Outright rejection of a belief in God. Popular perspective present in today's society.

Attentiveness

Continuous focus on God; spiritual attentiveness. See *"Nepsis."*

Body of Christ

An analogy of all believers united together in a single body with Christ Jesus as its head. A body has many members, but remains a single body (unity which retains diversity). Christ speaks of the unity all believers in his analogy of the vine and branches (John 15:1-10). Images of the Church as the body of Christ come from Rom. 12:5, 1 Cor. 12-27, Col. 1:18, 1:24, and Eph. 5:23. As such, the Church is one with Christ. See also *Koinonia*.

Boredom

Sad longing or emptiness; a sense of missing something to which we are attached. Previous pleasures or material things no longer satisfy the inner longing. Joy is elusive. A loss of energy, purpose, or zeal. Leads to despair, depression, despondency, and even burnout.

Charity

In the context of a theological virtue, we love God more than everything, and our neighbor for the love of God. See also *"Agapé."* Charity is one of the three theological virtues, along with faith and hope. Per St. Paul, charity (love) is the greatest of these virtues. See 1 Cor. 13:1-13.

Complacency

A feeling of uncritical satisfaction with oneself or one's achievements. In the spiritual journey, there is a danger of presuming one has made sufficient progress towards salvation wherein further effort is not required. Jesus warns against this in the Parable of the Rich Fool (Luke 12:16-21). Synonyms for complacency include self-satisfaction, self-approval, self-approbation, self-admiration, and self-congratulation. When a primary objective of the spiritual journey is surrender of self-will to the Divine will, just by its definition, one can see the dangers of complacency, wherein the focus is on "self."

Compunction

Regret or remorse for sinfulness. See *Penthos*.

Contemplation

Refers to various practices that aim at "looking at," "gazing at," or "being aware of" God or the divine presence. Contemplative prayer follows meditation and is the highest form of prayer that aims to achieve a close spiritual union with God.

Conversion

Transformation or change of heart, *metanoia* (μετάνοια). For most, conversion is an ongoing, life-long process and not a "big bang" one-time event. We must continually choose to follow Jesus on a daily basis. ("If anyone wishes to come after me, he must deny himself and take up his cross *daily* and follow me" – Luke 9:23).

Deification	See "Divinization." These terms are used interchangeably.
Delusion	See "Spiritual Delusion."
Deposit of Faith *(Depositum Fidei)*	The content of divine revelation (revealed truth) coming to us from the Sacred Scriptures and Sacred Tradition. Combined, these are a single Deposit of Faith that form the basis of our Catholic beliefs. It is considered sacred because it comes from God, and a deposit because it has been left to us by Christ.
Desert Spirituality	Spirituality drawing predominantly from the lives of the Desert Fathers and Mothers from the Early Church. This includes the hesychast prayer tradition (Jesus Prayer) and spiritual disciplines such as ascetical practices, detachment, mourning our sinfulness, and a spirit of penance. Throughout the history of Eastern Christian Spirituality, the Ancient Church to modern times, one can observe that it is deeply rooted in Desert Spirituality. That is one reason we call this a "back-to-basics" spirituality—simple yet continuously relevant to the spiritual journey and personal holiness.
Desire	See "Longing."
Despair	A complete loss or absence of hope. The Good News of the Gospel is intended to give us hope, that a life of eternal blessedness awaits us. However, the demons try to exploit our weaknesses in order to diminish our hope.

Despondency
A state in which one's spirits are low, reflecting a loss of hope or courage. It is one of the weaknesses the demons try to exploit in order to disrupt our relationship with God. As St. Seraphim of Sarov wrote: "Despondency is a worm gnawing the heart."[407]

Detachment
From the Greek *apatheia* (ἀπάθεια), a state of mind free from passions, such as a movement of the soul toward irrational love or senseless hate. In order to grow in the spiritual life, especially in contemplative prayer, a person must strive for personal purification in order to be freed from the passions and attain the virtues. *Apatheia* is a state of total dependence on God's grace— It is only possible to attain through *synergeia*.

Diakonia
(διακονία)
Greek term meaning "service." In theological terms, it is a call to serve the poor and oppressed. The call of the first "deacons" in Acts 6:6, was to take care of the Greek widows, who were neglected in the daily distribution of bread. So, first and foremost, this concept is about serving the poor and marginalized. It is the type of heart and mindset to which all followers of Jesus should aspire. See also "Almsgiving."

Dispassion
Free from or unaffected by the passions. This is the foundation from which to cultivate the virtues. Some Holy Fathers refer to three stages in the spiritual life. The first is to conquer the passions or eliminate them entirely (see "Passions"). This creates the foundation to cultivate the virtues.

Distractions
From the Greek *logismoi* (λογίσμοι), invading or intrusive thoughts that disturb or sidetrack one in prayer. One must always be vigilant (*nepsis*) in order to maintain inner stillness (*hesychia*).

---

407 Zander, *St. Seraphim of Sarov*, 103.

Divine   When used as a noun, the Divine refers to God. For example, we speak about encountering "the Divine." Used as a noun, it is capitalized herein.

Divine Attributes   The attributes of God that we infer from our experience of God and the teachings of Jesus. These include goodness, love, mercy, compassion, long-suffering, patience, purity, and having pure love for neighbor. *Theosis* is the process by which the human person gradually becomes divinized (deified) by practicing the divine attributes (also called the God-like virtues) in order to fulfill our destiny: union with God.

Divine Image   How humanity is created (see "Image of God"). "God created mankind in his image; in the image of God he created them; male and female he created them" (Gen. 1:27). Early Church Fathers would say that we are patterned after the Image Absolute, which is Jesus Christ.

Divine Liturgy   See "Liturgy."

Divine Office   Official set of prayers of the Church, marking the hours of each day and sanctifying the day with prayer. With the liturgy, it constitutes the official public prayer life of the Church. Matins and Vespers are two examples of specific hours or "offices" that are prayed. There are also Little Hours in between: First, Second, Third, Sixth, etc. In the Eastern Churches, the book of hours is called the *Horologion* (Ὡρολόγιον), which literally means "the hour-teller." The equivalent in the Roman Church is the breviary or *The Liturgy of the Hours*.

Divine Presence	The presence of God. It is this presence that we experience in prayer and in our lives when we remain spiritually attuned. In Eastern Christian Spirituality, sometimes this is referred as experiencing the "energies" or "operations" of God (see "Energies.")
Divinization	Related to the concept of *theosis*, the process of practicing the God-like virtues, becoming more "God-like," in order to prepare ourselves for our destiny: union with God.
Elder	A Spiritual Father. See "*Staretz*."
Encounter	To come upon or meet with. In the context used herein, the premise is that God is meant to be experienced in a tangible way. "The Joy of the Gospel fills the hearts and lives of all who encounter Jesus" (Pope Francis, *Evangelii Gaudium*, no. 1).
Energies	The operations of God that can be experienced and that allow us to know something about God. These are considered "uncreated energies" because they are actions of God in the world. From the Greek *energeia* (ἐνέργεια).
Enlightenment (Divine Illumination)	The divine assistance or grace that we are provided to discern whether our thoughts and actions are aligned with the Divine will, and to gain greater insights with respect to the divine mysteries generally based on contemplation or encounters with the Divine Presence. Sometimes referred to as Holy Illumination. Not to be confused with the philosophical movement known as The Enlightenment (see below).

Enlightenment (Philosophical)
An intellectual and philosophical movement that dominated the ideas of Europe in the eighteenth century. It fostered a belief in the inherent goodness of humanity and confidence that human beings had the capacity for greatness within themselves, dismissing the role of God (reason over faith). Over time, this spawned several other movements or philosophical schools of thought including Humanism, Rationalism, and Individualism. See below. All of these schools of thought, which have influenced our culture today, illustrate a movement away from God and even communal responsibilities, with an increased focus on self. Accordingly, within our secular society we have developed a culture of individualism, which subconsciously influences our perspectives and actions.

Essence
The inward nature, true substance, or constitution of anything. God in his essence is a mystery and, as such, unknowable. However, we can learn something about God through our experience of his operations (energies). From the Greek *ousia* (οὐσία), meaning "essence" or "substance."

Humans cannot comprehend the essence or nature of God, nor can we take on the essence. However, we can share in, partake of, or participate in the divine nature as we strive to be more like God; striving to live the virtues. This involves self-surrender of our will to the divine will, which prepares us for our destiny: union with God.

Eternal Blessedness
To live in union with God, which is our human purpose or destiny. Sometimes this is also referred to as "communion with God," sharing in the very life of the Holy Trinity. *Theosis* is the incremental process of striving to prepare ourselves for this destiny.

147

Faith

Confidence or trust in a person or thing. Herein, faith refers to confidence and trust in God. Faith is one of the three theological virtues, along with hope and charity (love) — gifts from God that lead us to him and allow us to live in closer relationship with him.

Fall

Term used to describe the sin of Adam and Eve, rejecting dependence on God (preferring self over God), and represents the transition from a state of innocent obedience to God to one of disobedience. The Fall created a defect in human nature, enslaving humanity to sin and making us more susceptible to temptation. Said another way, humanity was made in the image and likeness of God (Gen. 1:27), but lost the likeness through the sin of Adam and Eve. As sung in the Troparion for the Pre-Festive Day of the Nativity: "Christ is born to raise up the likeness that had fallen."

Fallen Nature

As a consequence of the Fall, human nature has been gravely weakened, enslaved to sin, and susceptible to temptation. Through the Incarnation, our human nature was restored to its original nobility. Through Baptism, we are granted new life and the possibility of life with God in heaven. However, we must continually strive to renew our restored nature through our daily, incremental efforts (*theosis*). Some spiritual writers explain that unless we understand the depth of our fallen nature, our true humanity (our "sinful nature"), we will not understand our need for salvation. Further, by coming to understand our fallen nature, we will be more likely to mourn our sinfulness (*penthos*).

Fasting   Ascetical/penitential practice of abstaining from food, creating a physical hunger and being reminded of the spiritual void only Christ can fill. If we fast with our heart, we express our love for God and acknowledge our sinfulness. Our sacrifice unites us to the sacrifice of Jesus Christ, who shed his blood for our salvation. Further, self-denial disposes us to freedom from worldly distractions to create an environment conducive to prayer. Through voluntary fasting, we unite ourselves in solidarity with the poor and suffering who have no food, being reminded that we are all members of the Body of Christ, and are reliant upon God for all our blessings.

Fear of the Lord   A reverential fear or awe of God in his majesty. It is not a phobia or a negative fear. It implies a rightly ordered relationship between God (Creator) and the person (created). Fear of the Lord is considered one of the seven gifts of the Holy Spirit. Fear of God is used interchangeably herein. As St. Isaac the Syrian wrote, "The fear of God is the beginning of virtue."

Forgetfulness   Loss of spiritual attentiveness or zeal; complacency. Places the soul at risk. See "*Nepsis.*"

Forgiveness   From the Greek *aphesis* (ἄφεσις), meaning "dismissal" or "release" or figuratively "pardon." Forgiveness frees the mind from anger and resentment, demons that can impair our interior stillness. Jesus tells the Parable of the Unforgiving Servant (Matt. 18:21-35) and concludes by saying, "So will my Heavenly Father do to you, unless each of you forgives his brother from his heart" (Matt. 18:35). Note the emphasis on *heart*, which means genuine forgiveness versus superficial and is intended to assist one in remaining "clean of heart," an important concept in *theosis.*

149

Formation The process of forming or the state of being formed. In the context used herein, formation is the spiritual grounding of an individual (experiential based on encounter) as opposed to catechesis, which is formal instruction, based on an academic approach to theology (intellectual knowledge). Thus, formation is coming to know and entering into a relationship with Jesus Christ, learning to live our lives with him as our guide (learning to become more Christ-like) versus solely an intellectual understanding of doctrines of faith. As Isaac the Syrian would say, "You cannot taste honey by reading a book." See also *"Praxis."*

Freedom The state of being free or at liberty without confinement or under physical restraint; exemption from external control, interference, regulation, etc.; the power to determine action without restraint. Surrender of self-will to the Divine will is an act of freedom.

God-like Virtues See "Divine Attributes."

Hesychia (ἡουχία) Stillness, watchfulness, interior silence of the heart. Hesychast prayer, also known more commonly as the Jesus Prayer, is a contemplative prayer practice. Hesychasm evolved from the practices of the Desert Fathers and Mothers during the third to seventh centuries, and was further developed in the monasteries on Mount Athos during the Greek Spiritual Renaissance (1200-1400). It advanced further in Russia during the Russian Spiritual Renaissance (1700-1917) and is still faithfully preserved and practiced within the Eastern Christian Churches, both Catholic and Orthodox. Also called "Prayer of the Heart."

Holiness   The state in which we strive to fulfill our destiny, which is union with God. It is an ongoing journey of transformation involving spiritual struggle and increasing devotion to God. See also "Universal Call to Holiness."

Holy Mysteries   Term used by the Eastern Churches for Sacraments. Comes from the Greek *mystērion* (μυστήριον), meaning "mystery." Emphasis is placed on the mystery of the ritual. The "holy mysteries" are considered vessels for mystical participation in divine grace.

Hope   The combination of a desire for something and an expectation of receiving it. St. Paul writes that hope is for that which is unseen (Rom. 8:24) and the ultimate hope is in our supernatural destiny of union with God. It is hope that brings us to desire eternal life as our ultimate happiness. "And hope does not disappoint," as St. Paul wrote (Rom. 5:5). Hope is one of the three theological virtues along with faith and charity (love).

Human Heart   A commonly held belief, beginning with the Early Desert Fathers and Mothers, is that Christianity was a divinizing process taking place gradually within the human heart, the interior focus where man and the Triune God meet.

Humility   From the earth; grounded. A simple, low opinion of one's self, avoiding honors, ranks, titles. It is the foundation for the other virtues.

Humanism   An outlook or system of thought attaching prime importance to human rather than divine or supernatural matters. This is a movement away from God spawned by the Enlightenment.

Image of God	The sum total of our possibilities. It is imprinted upon us and can never be taken away. As humans, we have a capacity for God (*capex Dei*) and the ability to enter into relationship with him because we are related to him. In this context, we describe ourselves as being created in the divine image.
Incarnation	The doctrine that the second person of the Trinity, the *Logos*, assumed human form in the person of Jesus Christ and is completely God and completely man without mixture or confusion. Renowned 20th century Catholic Theologian Karl Rahner, SJ, uses the term: "divinized humanity," essentially describing our goal as humans—divinization (i.e., *theosis*).
Individualism	(1) The habit or principle of being independent and self-reliant and (2) a social theory favoring freedom of action for individuals over collective or state control. This is a movement away from God spawned by the Enlightenment.
Indwelling Divine Presence	The presence of the Divine within the human heart. Through Baptism, we have the Indwelling Presence. We cultivate this presence by following the example of Jesus, through self-surrender, and aligning our will with the Divine will.
Interior Monasticism	For a non-monastic, adopting certain monastic practices such as prayer and spiritual disciplines (repentance, asceticism, and detachment), designed to deepen one's relationship with God. See also, "Art of Spiritual Life."
Interior Stillness	See "*Hesychia*."
Interior Struggle	See "Unseen Warfare."

Jesus Prayer

A prayer tradition emerging from Desert Spirituality, focused on interior stillness in order to encounter the presence of God. One of the most popular forms of the prayer is "Lord Jesus Christ, Son of God, have mercy on me, a sinner." See "*Hesychia*."

Kathara Proseuche (καθαρή προσευχή)

This is the third and highest level of participation in prayer according to the hesychast tradition following praxis and *theoria*. See "Pure Prayer."

Kenosis (κένωσις)

Renunciation of the divine nature, at least in part, by Christ in the Incarnation: "Who, though he was in the form of God, did not deem equality with God something to be grasped. Rather, he emptied himself, taking the form of a slave" (Phil. 2:6-7). This should be contrasted to Adam, who wanted to be "like God" (the temptation). Thus, Jesus models for us the right relationship with God (dependent through self-emptying).

Koinonia (κοινωνία)

Christian fellowship or communion or joint participation with God or, more commonly, with fellow Christians.

Lectio Divina

Latin for "Divine Reading." A traditional Benedictine practice of scriptural reading, meditation, and prayer to promote communion with God and to increase the knowledge of God's Word. Lectio Divina has four steps: read; meditate; pray; and contemplate. A passage of Scripture is read, then its meaning reflected upon. This is followed by prayer and contemplation on the Word of God. The focus is not a theological analysis of biblical passages, but rather viewing Christ as the living Word of God. This illustrates how Sacred Scripture can be a means of encounter.

Levels of Prayer   Participation or depth of encounter, noting also the difference between beginners and experienced practitioners. In the Christian East, these levels are generally referred to as *praxis*, *theoria*, and *kathara proseuche* or pure prayer. In Western spirituality, comparable levels are defined: purgative, illuminative, and unitive. In both cases, the highest level of participation (pure or unitive prayer) involves an experience of union with God and is only granted by God to the practitioner based on his or her effort. Those who have achieved this highest level of prayer are often referred to as mystics.

Lex orandi, lex credendi   Latin, loosely meaning "the law of prayer is the law of believing." This expresses the thought that Tradition handed on to us such as Liturgy points to the beliefs held by the earliest disciples and, thus, gives us an indication of their beliefs and theology. It is an explanation of the importance placed on Tradition as a source of divine inspiration, drawing on how people lived their beliefs.

Likeness of God   Image of God's fulfillment, our ability to become who God wants us to be, achieving our possibilities, bringing us to our purpose: eternal blessedness. As discussed above, means to live ultimately in union with him—nothing less. We may choose not to seek to achieve our possibilities, but the Image of God can never be taken from us.

Listlessness   Reflective of a lack of energy, drive, or purpose. In the absence of hope, many find themselves drifting through life without a sense of purpose or meaning. The Good News of the Gospel is that humanity does have a purpose; we are created in the image of God to share eternal blessedness with him. God alone can fulfill our deepest longing.

Liturgy "Work of the people," from the Greek *liturgeia* (λιτυργεια). Eastern Christian Eucharistic worship is generally called the Divine Liturgy, reflecting how heaven and earth come together in worship.

Logismoi (λογίσμοι) See "Distractions."

Longing A desire in every human heart that aspires to something more. Every person has a desire for happiness and fulfillment, to love and be loved. Longing is a spiritual void created by God in humans so that he alone can fill it with his love. Anything else by which we try to fill that longing just creates temporary fulfillment that, once the feeling of fulfillment has passed, often results in dissatisfaction and frustration. That is because we attempt to fill infinite longing with finite things. As part of the spiritual journey, we come to an increased realization that our longing is truly for the Divine Presence and that we can only be who we were created to be through him. He alone can fill our deepest longing.

Love (*Agapé*) The highest form of love, charity; the love of God for man and of man for God. This is contrasted to *eros* (ἔρως) or romantic love, *philía* (φιλία), which is love as a bond of friendship, and *storgē* (στοργή), which is love as a bond of empathy.

Martyr From the Greek *mártys* (μάρτυς), meaning "witness." The Church describes two types of martyrdom. Red martyrdom refers to those who voluntarily suffer and give their lives for their faith. White martyrdom refers to those who sacrifice through ascetical practices, like hermits and early monks of the Egyptian desert, bearing witness to their faith by the way they live.

Meditation	A form of prayer in which a structured attempt is made to become aware of and reflect upon the revelations of God.
Metanoia **(μετάνοια)**	True change of heart; conversion. Change in one's way of life resulting from penitence or spiritual conversion. Consider the example of Zacchaeus. (See Luke 19:1–10). See also "Conversion." Such change is brought about in the human heart by divine grace.[408] (See *synergeia*.)
Mountaintop **Experience**	Expression for an intense spiritual experience. These are infrequent and granted by God as gifts based on the needs of the individual.
Mourning our **Sinfulness**	See "*Penthos*."
Mount Athos	The epicenter of Eastern Orthodox monastic spirituality. Mount Athos is a mountain and peninsula in Greece, the location of 20 significant monasteries under the direct jurisdiction of the Ecumenical Patriarch of Constantinople. The term "Athonite" refers to Mount Athos.
Mystic	One who has had an experience of the Divine. Herein, we have discussed having an awareness of the presence of God. The adjective is "mystical." As Rahner wrote, "The devout Christian of the future will either be a 'mystic,' one who has 'experienced' something, or he [she] will cease to be anything at all."
Mysticism	Becoming one with God; mystical union or direct communion with God. This occurs when one achieves pure prayer or unitive prayer. Not all will achieve this height of prayer because it is a gift granted by God commensurate with one's efforts.

---

408 See St. Theophan the Recluse, *The Path to Salvation*, 87.

Nature The basic, real, and invariable nature of a thing or its significant individual feature or features. Humanity's union with God is a union of two distinct natures (human and divine).

Nepsis (Νιψις) Sober vigilance and spiritual attentiveness. As a person draws closer to God, it is important to remain vigilant for assaults from the Evil One, which often can be subtle and try to intervene in our relationship with God. Also called "sobriety" by the Holy Fathers, loss of which leads to forgetfulness, loss of zeal, and complacency. Without sobriety, temptations and evil suggestions approach the door of the heart and, finding it unguarded, enter and bring with them a whole swarm of unclean thoughts that darken the mind and heart. "To keep silence as you should and to be sober in your heart, let the Jesus Prayer cleave to your breath—and in a few days you will see it in practice."[409]

New Evangelization *Millennio Ineunte* (2001). It is an invitation for all Catholics to renew their relationship with Jesus Christ and his Church, for each person to deepen his or her faith, have confidence in the Gospel, and possess a willingness to share the Gospel. It begins with a personal encounter with Jesus. In turn, renewed by our encounter, we are called to reach out to the baptized who have fallen away from Church. Pope Benedict XVI clarified that the New Evangelization is new, not in its content, but new in its inner thrust and methods to confront the cultural crisis created by secularization.

Nouvelle Théologie French for "new theology." See *"ressourcement."*

---

409 Hesychius of Jerusalem, "Texts on Sobriety and Prayer." Taken from *Writings from the Philokalia on Prayer of the Heart*, transl. E. Kadloubovsky and G.E.H. Palmer (London: Faber and Faber, 1992), 316.

Nous (νόος)	Equated to intellect or intelligence; the rational mind; the rational part of the soul. In hesychast prayer, practitioners place the *nous* into the heart in order to avoid distractions and achieve stillness. This is the reason the prayer practice is also called "Prayer of the Heart." *Noetic* is the adjective and sometimes this method of prayer is called noetic prayer.
Operations of God	God acting within his creation in which he reveals himself to us. Romanian Orthodox Theologian Dumitru Stăniloae called these "new acts that guide creation" for "the needs we have at each moment."[410] It is through his operations, that we can experience God and infer something about God, such as his divine attributes. See also "Divine Presence" and "Energies."
Passions	Sinful habits or demons that challenge us, trying to prevent us from cultivating the God-like virtues that will lead us to eternal blessedness. These include pride, lust, anger, greed, unfaithfulness, envy, sloth, ingratitude, and indifference. We are inclined to the passions because of our fallen nature. In our spiritual journey, we struggle to conquer these passions (see "Unseen Warfare"). We cannot overcome these on our own, many of which are deeply ingrained in our human nature. Rather, this requires human-divine collaboration (*synergeia*).

---

410 See Dumitru Stăniloae, *Revelation and Knowledge of the Triune God*. Taken from "The Experience of God" series, vol. 1, transl. Ioan Ionita and Robert Barringer (Brookline, MA: Holy Cross Orthodox Press, 1998), 126. "Through his attributes God makes something of his being evident to us, but this something is made specific within one vast and uninterrupted symphony of continually new acts that guide creation and each element of it separately towards the final goal of union with him."

Patristics

Reference to Early Church Fathers, both Latin and Greek, and their writings. The Patristic Period began at the end of the Apostolic Period (time of the Apostles, ca. 100). For the Western Church, the Patristic Period ends after the Second Council of Nicaea (787), the last of the First Seven Ecumenical Councils of the undivided Church. This period is considered significant because consensus was reached through these councils on the primary doctrines of the Church. Through a movement leading up to the Second Vatican Council, the concept of *ressourcement*, a return to the sources, generally means a return to the teachings of Sacred Scripture and the Church Fathers. Also, the Eastern Church considers this Patristic Period to have extended into the fifteenth century through Simeon of Thessalonica, as evidenced by the writers included in Migne's *Patrologia Graeca*.

Pelagianism

Heresy in the Early Church, named after the British monk Pelagius (354-420), who taught that humanity could choose the good and achieve salvation through individual efforts and, most notably, *without* divine assistance.

***Penthos* (πένθος)**

Also called compunction, this is mourning our sinfulness ("Spare your people, O Lord") and an important part of repentance as a state of mind. Some Greek Fathers also describe the gift of tears associated with such mourning, a reflection of unworthiness, and a desire for the mercy of God. This also helps to cultivate the virtue of humility.

Personal Holiness

See "Universal Call to Holiness."

Prayer

Spending time with God, entering more deeply into relationship with him. While there are many forms of prayer, our primary focus herein has been on contemplation and *hesychia* (hesychast prayer/Jesus Prayer). Other types of prayer include liturgical prayer and recitation of the Divine Office. Prayer is considered a penitential practice in terms of returning to God, rending our hearts, and acknowledging our sinfulness. Through prayer, we begin to establish a right-ordered relationship between us and our Creator.

Praxis (πρᾶξις)

The process by which a theory, lesson, or skill is enacted, practiced, embodied, or realized. This is true in the spiritual life as we live our lives in conformity with Christ, adopting his teachings and the lessons he modeled for us, and reinforced through prayer. Like any skill that we desire to perfect, we must continually practice and remain steadfast in our efforts. Thus, our vocation to holiness is brought to life.

In the hesychast tradition, this is considered the first level of participation in prayer. It involves the active struggle through ascetical practices, living the virtues, and other spiritual practices such as repentance and mourning our sinfulness (*penthos*) in order to achieve personal purification. This is the foundation for further levels of participation in prayer. *Praxis* can lead to *theoria*.

Prelest

See "Spiritual Delusion."

Pure Prayer   This is the highest level of participation according to the hesychast prayer tradition. It is an experience of union with God in peace, love, and joy occurring in this present life. This level of participation is a gift from God and is not given to all. Those who have achieved this level of participation describe intense feelings and an experience of light. Under the teachings of St. Gregory Palamas, this is an experience of Tabor Light (light experienced by the apostles at the Transfiguration of Jesus on Mount Tabor).

Purification   To purify, refine, and be set free from any impurities that could contaminate our lives. Consider how gold is refined by fire, increasingly removing impurities, and becoming more valuable. The same is true in pursuing our vocation to holiness. This is indicative of our incremental journey of transformation, preparing ourselves for eternal blessedness (union with God, sharing in the life of the Holy Trinity). See also "Conversion," "Deification," "Divinization," "*Metanoia*," "Sanctification," "*Theosis*," and "Transformation."

Rationalism   A belief or theory that opinions and actions should be based on reason and knowledge rather than on religious belief or emotional response. This is a movement away from God spawned by the Enlightenment.

Relativism   Belief that there is no absolute truth such as expressed by Christianity. Popular perspective present in today's society.

Religious Pluralism   Belief that there is more than one path to holy and ethical living. Popular perspective in today's society, which stands in opposition to the Christian faith.

Remembrance of Death

To regularly recall the inevitability of our own death, wherein at some point we will stand before the fearsome judgment seat of Christ. Through this reflection, we begin to appreciate the need for our salvation, which in turn increases reverential fear of God (humility) and realization that our own merits are bankrupt. We begin to increasingly appreciate our need for divine mercy. The Jesus Prayer and remembrance of death, in essence, converge. From the prayer comes a vivid remembrance of death, as if it were a foretaste of it; and from this foretaste of death the prayer itself flares up more urgently.

As an example of this remembrance, in one of the Prayers before Sleep, there is the Prayer of St. John of Damascus, which begins:

> O Lord, Lover of Mankind, is this bed to be my coffin or will you enlighten my wretched soul with another day? Here the coffin lies before me, and here death confronts me. I fear, O Lord, your judgment and the endless torments; yet I cease not to do evil …[411]

Remembrance of God

Mnimi Theou (Μνήμη Θεού). Essentially a constant presence to God, as he is to us. We do not take God for granted or lose sight of him. In the hesychast prayer tradition, this is generally accomplished through the regular invocation of the Jesus Prayer. As St. Ignatius Brianchaninov wrote, "The benefit of remembrance of God is unquantifiable."[412]

---

411 *Publicans Prayer Book*, 3rd ed. (Boston: Sophia Press, 2017), 89-90.
412 Brianchaninov, *The Refuge*, 161.

Repentance

This is both the Holy Mystery of Repentance (Sacrament of Confession) and our interior disposition of mourning our sinfulness, realizing our need for God and salvation. Jesus began his ministry with the message: "Repent, for the kingdom of heaven is at hand" (Matt. 4:17). Accordingly, when we discuss the Jesus Prayer, part of the *praxis* is to develop a penitential mindset, recognizing the reality that we are sinners and in need of God's mercy.

Ressourcement

French for a "return to the sources." This was a movement by French and German theologians that included a renewed interest in biblical exegesis, mysticism, and Patristics. One could say that this was a return to the basics. This movement is also called *Nouvelle Théologie* (New Theology), a counterpoint to the dominant dogmatic theology that existed prior to the Second Vatican Council (Scholasticism). This focus on a return to the sources had a significant influence on the Council. See Patristics.

Rule of Prayer

The outline of our daily prayer routine—a structured rule that is practiced each day. It should specify a time, generally morning and evening, and, if possible, a place for prayer. As with any skill, prayer is something that should be practiced regularly.

Sacraments

Term used by the Western Church from the Latin, *sacramentum,* meaning "sign of the sacred." The Sacraments are considered to have a visible and invisible reality—a reality open to the human senses (visible) but grasped in its God-given depths with the eyes of faith (invisible).

Salvation   The goal of Christianity and the purpose of the Church, allowing us to come to know and love Jesus Christ in order to share eternal blessedness with God in heaven. Having our likeness restored to its original nobility, the human person strives to follow the example of Jesus, to become more Christ-centric, in order to achieve this goal. Striving occurs through incremental efforts (see *"Theosis"*), which is how a person is divinized (see "Divinization") in preparation for his or her destiny: union with God. Salvation cannot be achieved through individual efforts, but requires divine-human collaboration (*synergeia*).

Sanctification   By definition, to make holy, to purify, or to free from sin. In pursuing a vocation to holiness, we are sanctifying our lives in order to prepare ourselves for eternal blessedness. It is a deliberate choice, saying "yes" to Christ, and an ongoing process of purification. See also *"Theosis."*

Secular Humanism   See "Humanism."

Secularism   Humanistic values that allow a life of ethical integrity without faith. In other words, faith is not necessary in order for one to live a good life. Popular perspective present in today's society, which stands in opposition to the Christian faith.

Self-Activating Prayer   When the Jesus Prayer has become so internalized that the heart begins to pray the words on its own, even in one's sleep. This is a high-level of participation in the Prayer and a gift granted by God.

Self-surrender   Same as self-denial. We freely choose to surrender our own will (self-will) to the Divine will. Jesus says to be his disciple, one must deny himself, take up his cross daily, and follow him (Cf. Luke 9:23). See also *Kenosis*.

Sinful Nature   Human nature with an inclination towards sin as a consequence of the Fall (sin of Adam and Eve). See "Fallen Nature."

Sober Vigilance   Spiritual attentiveness. Also referred to as "sobriety." See "*Nepsis*."

Sobornost   Term that evolved during the Russian Spiritual Renaissance in the 1800s, it emphasizes the cooperation of people over individualism. The image used to illustrate this concept is the parish church in the middle of the village, drawing all people together and helping to provide for the needs of all, first and foremost being the spiritual needs.

Spiritual Accompaniment   Joining together as a community of pilgrims on our journey to draw closer to God. As Pope Francis wrote, we support one another, "removing our sandals before others in humility," walking with each other "in a steady and reassuring manner, reflecting our closeness and a compassionate gaze which heals, liberates, and encourages our growth in the Christian life" (*Evangelii Gaudium*, no. 169). Spiritual accompaniment is important because as pilgrims on a journey, we are no longer orphaned, helpless, and homeless. We are not drifters, because communally we have a sense of direction with the desire to draw closer to God.

Spiritual Delusion   Disordered perceptions about personal sanctity or progress on the spiritual journey. This generally is the result of pride or vainglory that can encroach upon the person or belief that personal exertion can achieve progress. It can also manifest itself as complacency ("I am doing well enough compared to others"), which is also a form of pride. In essence, it is a loss of humility and a loss of the sense of dependency on God. At all points along the spiritual journey, the pilgrim must remain completely dependent on God (*synergeia*).

Spiritual Direction   The practice of accompanying people as they attempt to deepen their relationship with the Divine, or to grow in their own personal holiness. The companion (or spiritual director) accompanies the directee and is generally a Spiritual Father or Mother, often a priest, monk, or nun. See also "Elder" and "*Staretz*."

Spiritual Warfare   See "Unseen Warfare."

Stillness   See "*Hesychia*."

Starchestvo   A lineage of spiritual wisdom maintained by an elder (*staretz*). The Greek and Russian monastic traditions have a long unbroken history of elders and disciples, often centered on certain monasteries (Athonite, Optina, Pechersk Lavra, etc.). This was how the hesychast tradition was transmitted from one generation to the next.

Staretz   A spiritual elder from whom people seek spiritual guidance. For example, beginning in the Russian Spiritual Renaissance, lay-people would come to the monastery for spiritual counsel. An elder may also have disciples who place themselves in obedience to him. See *starchestvo*.

Struggle   See "Unseen Warfare."

Synergeia   Greek for "synergy." This is the relationship
(συνεργεια)   between Divine grace and human freedom;
                               the person's collaboration with the Divine
                               to achieve his or her final destiny. God does
                               not force his grace upon us, but guides and
                               strengthens us when we submit to his will
                               (self-surrender). As Jesus said, "No one can
                               come to me unless the Father who sent me
                               draw him, and I will raise him on the last day"
                               (John 6:44). It is about divine initiative and the
                               human response to that initiative.

                               People cannot achieve salvation without divine
                               assistance. Jesus told us, "Without me, you
                               can do nothing" (John 15:5). Pelagianism was
                               a heresy that taught humanity could achieve
                               salvation through their individual efforts. Pope
                               Francis warned against modern Pelagianism in
                               his apostolic exhortation, *Gaudete et Exsultate*.

Theologia   Theology generally means the study of God.
(θεολογία)   However, *theologia* in this sense means
                               a relationship with God that transcends
                               knowledge. In other words, we learn something
                               about God through our experiences of God. The
                               human provides the desire, making the free-will
                               choice, and God gives the grace so that through
                               this collaboration, our destiny of union with
                               God can be achieved. It is also an emphasis on
                               the fact that this is not an intellectual endeavor;
                               rather, it is based on relationship and experience.
                               There is a well-known axiom in Eastern Christian
                               spirituality taken from the writings of Evagrius
                               Ponticus: "If you are a theologian you truly pray.
                               If you truly pray you are a theologian."

Theological Virtues See "Virtues."

Theoria (θεωρία)	The second level of participation in prayer, according to the hesychast tradition. This is contemplation of God, gaining a greater sense of his presence. It is based on establishing the proper foundation through praxis. See *"praxis."*
Theosis (Θέωσις)	Divinization or deification. The ongoing process of transformation or conversion wherein we increasingly practice the God-like virtues in order to prepare for our destiny: union with God. See 2 Pet. 1:4, "[Jesus] has bestowed on us the precious and very great promises, so that through them you may come to share in the divine nature ..." *Theosis* is a process that begins in our temporal life and culminates in the life to come at the Resurrection of the Dead. Essentially, *theosis* is the core of the Good News of the Gospel, namely that we are called to share in the very life of God. It is the affirmative response to God, who communicates himself to us.
Theotokos (Θεοτόκος)	Greek term meaning "God-bearer." Title of the Blessed Virgin Mary given to her at the Council of Ephesus (431). From this, we derive the term "Mother of God." Note that Mary was declared the *Theotokos* (God-bearer), not *Christotokos* (Christ-bearer), reinforcing the proper understanding of the Incarnation of Jesus Christ, who was both fully human and fully divine. The term *Theotokos* is often used in Eastern Christian prayers (e.g., "through the prayers of the *Theotokos*, O Savior save us").
Transcendence	The state of going beyond ordinary limits; surpassing; exceeding. Each human person has a desire for something greater, something that derives purpose and meaning.

Transformation The ongoing process of conversion in order to achieve our destiny: union with God. See *"Theosis," "Metanoia,"* and "Conversion."

Trisagion Also known as the "Thrice Holy Hymn." It is a standard hymn or prayer for most Divine Liturgies of the Eastern Churches and included in most of the Hours as well. The words are: "Holy God, Holy and Mighty, Holy and Immortal, have mercy on us" (said three times with reverential bows each time).

Uncreated Energies A term for the operations of God as described in the mystical tradition of the Christian East. The energies are deemed "uncreated," meaning they contain the essence of God, because if they were created, we would not have a direct experience of the Divine. St. Gregory Palamas differentiated uncreated energies between (1) grace, which is beneficial participation in the "effects" of the uncreated energies, and (2) light, which is experienced by certain mystics who are able to achieve the highest levels of prayer, a temporal experience of union with God in the present life. In our spiritual journey, we encounter these energies of God, which are how he makes his presence known and the divine assistance provided (*synergeia*).

Uncreated Grace Rahner's term for God's divine assistance to those who are striving to transcend their limitations (finiteness) in order to advance in the spiritual life. It is considered "uncreated" under his concept of "Giver as gift," whereby the gift of grace is the Giver himself (God). It is through our experiences of uncreated grace that we can know something about God.

Union with God Our human destiny. See "Eternal Blessedness."

Universal Call to Holiness

The belief that all people, regardless of vocation or status, are called to personal holiness, for we all have the same destiny: union with God. It is based on Jesus's teaching, "So be perfect, just as your Heavenly Father is perfect" (Matt. 5:48). This particular term was described in the Second Vatican Council's document, "Dogmatic Constitution on the Church" (*Lumen Gentium*), Chapter V, November 21, 1964. "All the faithful of Christ of whatever rank or status, are called to the fullness of the Christian life and to the perfection of charity ..." (no. 40). However, this concept is not new. We see evidence of this call already playing out in everyday life throughout the history of the Church. For example, already 200 years before the Second Vatican Council in Russia, lay-people, from peasants to nobility, came to the monasteries such as Optina or Sarov, seeking spiritual counsel from the monks.

Unseen Warfare

The interior struggles a person has with temptations and passions, as referenced by the Church Fathers and Mothers. Sometimes also called spiritual warfare. Divinization is an ongoing struggle, striving to move from self-centered, self-will to self-surrender to the Divine will. Sometimes the battle can be fierce, like the clash of tectonic plates (self-will and divine-will). Sometimes it can be more subtle, as weeds slowly creeping into a well-managed lawn (see Parable of the Weeds among the Wheat, Matt. 13:24-30) — a reminder of the importance of constant vigilance. The Spiritual Fathers and Mothers advise us that this is a lifelong struggle; the demons will exploit any opportunity or weakness to interfere in our relationship with God.

Vigilance　　　　Constant watchfulness against attacks from the Evil One. See "*Nepsis.*"

Virtues　　　　　Gifts from God that lead us to live in closer relationship with him. The three theological virtues (faith, hope, and charity) come from God and lead us to God. These virtues are discussed in 1 Cor. 13:1-13.

Vocation to Holiness　The universal call and invitation by God to eternal blessedness (salvation). People are called to this life and invited by Jesus to follow him, preparing ourselves through a lifetime of conversion, struggles (see "Unseen Warfare"), and transformation for our ultimate destiny: eternal blessedness (union with God). See also: "Universal Call to Holiness."

Warmth of Heart　Created through spiritual attentiveness and continuous recitation of the Jesus Prayer. The objective of the prayer is for the mind to descend into the heart, free of distractions. Thus, the concentration of all human power is centered into one place, the heart. Over time, with continued practice and attentiveness of the mind, the heart begins to gradually warm. Hesychasts often describe this warmth of heart, implying a specific sensation when the prayer is ongoing and the mind is focused. However, if attentiveness is diluted such as through distractions, the heart will cool. See "Distractions" and "*Nepsis*".

Watchfulness　　Term used by some spiritual writers for attentiveness or sober vigilance. See "*Nepsis.*"

*You will know the truth, and
the truth will set you free.
(John 8:32)*

Historical Perspective

Selected Christian Spiritual Traditions: East and West

These significant spiritual traditions within the Church include the names of selected key individuals and writings from the respective periods:

	East	West
	Monastic Origins of Spirituality	
200 – 800s	**Desert Spirituality** • St. Antony of Egypt (251-356) • Rule of St. Pachomius (292-348) • St. Macarius the Great (c.300-91) • Various monastic leaders from the Egyptian desert (330s-460s), *Sayings of the Desert Fathers (Apophthegmata Patrum)* • St. Barsanuphius the Great and St. John of Gaza (mid-6th century), *Letters* • St. Dorotheos of Gaza (d. 565), *Discourses and Sayings* • St. John Climacus (579-606), *The Ladder of Divine Ascent* • St. Isaac the Syrian (640-700), *Ascetical Homilies* • After the Islamic conquest of Egypt in seventh century, some monks moved from the Egyptian desert to Mount Athos	**Desert Spirituality Moves West** • St. Augustine of Hippo (354-430), *Confessions* • St. John Cassian (360-435), *Conferences* and *Institutes* • St. Benedict of Nursia (480-543), founder of the Benedictine Order (Rule of St. Benedict), beginnings of *Lectio Divina*.

	East	West
	East	**West**
900 – 1200	**Eastern Monastic Spirituality** • First monasteries established on Mount Athos, which ultimately becomes the center of Eastern Orthodox spirituality • St. Symeon the New Theologian (949-1022), monk of the Monastery of St. Mammas, Constantinople, *Discourses* • St. Anthony of Kiev (983-1073), founds Pechersk Lavra, the Monastery of the Caves (Kiev), bringing Athonite spirituality to Russia	**Western Monastic Spirituality** • St. Bruno (1030-1101), founds Carthusian order • Robert of Molesme (1028-1111), a Benedictine abbot, founds the Cistercian order (1098) • St. Bernard of Clairvaux (1090-1153), reforms the Cistercian order
	Spirituality in the Scholastic Period	
1200 – 1400	**Greek Renaissance – Jesus Prayer** • Mount Athos becomes epicenter of hesychast spirituality • St. Gregory of Sinai (c.1265-1346) • St. Gregory Palamas (1296-1359), *Triads* • Hesychast Controversy (1330-54) • St. Nicholas Cabasilas (1322-92), *The Life in Christ* and *Commentary on the Divine Liturgy* **Russia** • St. Sergius of Radonezh (1314-92), a hermit, founds Holy Trinity Monastery near Moscow • St. Sergius and St. Herman, Athonite monks, found the Valaam Monastery at Lake Ladoga (~1389) **Serbia and Romania** • Nicodemus of Tismana (c.1320-1406), a disciple of Athonite St. Gregory of Sinai, founds one monastery in Serbia and two in Romania in the hesychast tradition	**Age of Scholasticism** *Separation of Spirituality and Theology* • St. Dominic (1170-1221), founder of the Dominican Order • St. Francis of Assisi (1182-1226), founder of the Franciscan Order • John Van Ruysbroeck (1293-1381), Flemish Mysticism • St. Catherine of Sienna (1347-80) *Dialogue of Divine Providence* • Julian of Norwich (1342-1416), *Showings* • Anonymous *Cloud of Unknowing* (late 14th century, Carthusian); first reference to a practice later known as Centering Prayer • Thomas à Kempis (1380-1471), *Imitation of Christ*

	East	West
	Spirituality in the Age of Reformation	
1400 – 1800	**Hesychia in Russia** • St. Nil Sorsky (1433-1503), disciple of St. Sergius, represents school of spirituality focused on the hesychast spiritual movement (Jesus Prayer, study of scripture and patristics, silence, and living simply). Contemplative mystics. *Predanie* (The Tradition) and *Ustav* (The Monastic Rule). Considered a teacher of prayer. • St. Joseph Volotsky (1440-1515), another disciple of St. Sergius, represents a different school of spirituality focused on strict obligation of obedience to God, and meticulous observance of rituals and liturgical worship. Large monasteries with estates. • Rivalry emerged between the two schools with Volotsky's dominating and carrying favor with the Muscovite state. Hesychast spirituality disappears from public view in Russia for almost 200 years, until the Russian Spiritual Renaissance.	**Age of Reformation** **Ignatian Spirituality** • St. Ignatius of Loyola (1491-1556), founder of the Jesuits, *Spiritual Exercises* **Carmelite Spirituality in Spain** • St. Teresa of Ávila (1515-82), *Interior Castle* • St. John of the Cross (1542-91), *Dark Night of the Soul* and *Ascent of Mount Carmel* **Other Threads** • St. Philip Neri (1515-95), founder of the Congregation of the Oratory • Lorenzo Scupoli (1530-1610), *Spiritual Combat* • St. Francis de Sales (1567-1622), founder of the Salesians, *Introduction to the Devout Life* • Pierre de Bérulle (1575-1629), founder of the French Oratory • St. Vincent de Paul (1580-1660) and St. Louise de Marillac (1591-1660) • Armand Jean le Bouthillier de Rancé (1626-1700), concerned about laxity, reforms the Cistercians in 1664 and creates the Order of Cistercians of the Strict Observance (OCSO), also known as the Trappists • St. Paul of the Cross (1694-1775), founder of the Passionists in 1720 • St. Alphonsus Liguori (1696-1787), founder of the Redemptorists, *The Way of the Cross*

	East	West
	Spirituality in the Age of Reason	

1700 – 1917	**Russian Spiritual Renaissance**
	Athonite Developments
	• Kollyvades Movement –spiritual renewal emphasizing Patristic theology, liturgical life, and frequent reception of communion; reaction against the European Enlightenment
	• St. Nicodemos the Hagiorite (1749-1809), original Greek *Philokalia* (1782), *Unseen Warfare* (1796), and *The Handbook of Spiritual Counsel* (1801)
	Russia
	• Paisius Velichkovsky (1722-94) translates *Philokalia* into Slavonic
	  » Optina Monastery (~1750s), becomes a significant spirituality center through disciples of Paisius
	  » Optina Elders, renowned spiritual masters (*Staretz*)
	• Appearance of the *Starchestvo*, spiritual threads based on an elder (*Staretz*)
	• St. Tikhon of Zadonsk (1724-83)
	• St. Seraphim of Sarov (1754-1833)
	  » Sarov becomes a significant spirituality center
	• Laity embrace Jesus Prayer and monastic spiritual practices
	• Anonymous classic *The Pilgrim's Tale* (~1860s); earliest redaction from Optina Monastery
	• St. Ignatius Brianchaninov (1807-67), *The Field*, *The Arena*, and *The Refuge*
	• St. Theophan the Recluse (1815-94), *Unseen Warfare* (updated) and *Philokalia* (*Dobrotolubiye*)
	• St. John of Kronstadt (1829-1908), *My Life in Christ*
		Age of Reason
		• Jean-Baptiste Henri Lacordaire (1802-61), re-establishes the Dominican order in Post-Revolutionary France
		• Isaac Hecker (1819-88), co-founder of the Paulists, focuses on the evangelization of America
		Oxford Movement
		• Included a focus on writings of the Early Church (patristics) and mystical writers; recovery of an integrated spirituality (body, mind, and heart), interior transformation, and emphasis on the potential of union with God
		• Pre-cursor to *ressourcement*, leading into the Second Vatican Council
		• St. John Henry Newman (1801-90), key figure in the Oxford Movement; also a founder of two Oratories in the United Kingdom, Birmingham (1848) and London (1849)
		Carmelite Spirituality in France
		• St. Thérèse of Lisieux, OCD (1873-97), *Story of a Soul*
		• St. Elizabeth of the Trinity, OCD (1880-1906)

	East	West
	Spirituality in the Modern Age	
1917 – Today	**Flourishing of Hesychast Tradition** **Russia and Eastern Europe** • Post-Communism (~1990s), prolific growth in monasteries in Russia, Ukraine, Romania, and Bulgaria **Russia** • Valaam Monastery returned to Orthodox Church (1989), the "Athos of the North" **Bulgaria** • Elder Seraphim Aleksiev (1912-93), *The Meaning of Suffering, Strife and Reconciliation*, and *The Forgotten Medicine: The Mystery of Repentance* **Romania** • Burning Bush movement at Antim Monastery (1945-58), a gathering of spiritual fathers focused on the revival of the hesychast tradition • Fr. Dumitru Stăniloae (1903-93) translates the original Greek *Philokalia* into Romanian • Elder Cleopa Ilie of Sihastria (1912-98) • Elder Arsenie Papacioc (1914-2011) **Serbia (influenced by Optina/ Valaam)** • Elder Thaddeus of Vitovnica (1914-2003)	**Age of Modernity** *Nouvelle Théologie* **(1935-60)** • "New Theology," a movement of critical reaction to Neo-Scholasticism with a desire to return Catholic theology to the original sources (Sacred Scripture and Church Fathers), most notably within circles of French and German theologians • Renewed interest in biblical exegesis and mysticism • Pre-cursor to *ressourcement* and its influence on reforms at the Second Vatican Council. **Second Vatican Council (1962-65)** • *Lumen Gentium* includes "Universal Call to Holiness" (Nov. 21, 1964) **Trappist/Contemplative Outreach (Cistercian Spirituality)** • Thomas Merton, OCSO (1915-68), coined the term "Centering Prayer" • Thomas Keating, OCSO (1923-2018) • Basil Pennington, OCSO (1931-2005) • William Meninger, OCSO (1932-) **World Community for Christian Meditation ("WCCM")** • Fr. John Main, OSB (1926-82) • Fr. Laurence Freeman, OSB (1951-) **Other Contemplatives** • Charles de Foucauld (1858-1916), hermit in North Africa • St. Teresa Benedicta of the Cross (Edith Stein) (1891-1942) • Caryll Houselander (1901-54) • Catherine Doherty (1896-1985), *Poustinia* (1975) • Mother Teresa of Calcutta (1910-97)

	East	West

	Athonite Revival of *Hesychia*
	• St. Silouan the Athonite (1866-1938)
	  » Elder Sophrony of Essex (1896-1993), *We Shall See Him As He Is*
	• Elder Joseph the Hesychast (1897-1959)
	  » Elder Ephraim of Arizona (Philotheou) (1927-2019)
	• Elder Porphyrios of Kavsokalyvia (1906-91), *Wounded by Love*
	• Elder Paisios of Mount Athos (1924-94)
	• Elder Ephraim of Katounakia (1912-98)
	• Archimandrite Aimilianos of Simonopetra (1934-2019)
	• Beginning in 2000, resurgence of monasteries on Mount Athos (Greece)
	Egyptian Monastic Revival
	• Monastic revival beginning in 1969
	• Fr. Matthew the Poor (Fr. Matta El Meskeen) (1919-2006), *Orthodox Prayer Life*
	• Fr. Lazarus al Anthony, video interviews (e.g., *The Last Anchorite* and Coptic Youth Channel's series, *A Monk's Life*)
		Modern Spiritual Movements
		Predominantly lay movements, focusing on the call to holiness and renewal, generally drawing together contemplation with action (evangelization, social justice); many focus on navigating the path to holiness within secular culture. Became increasingly popular after the Second Vatican Council and its teaching on the Universal Call to Holiness. Some of the more prominent examples, along with the founders, country of origin, and founding year, include:
		• Schoenstatt Movement (Fr. Joseph Kentenich, Germany, 1914)
		• Opus Dei (Fr. Josemaría Escrivá, Spain, 1928)
		• Catholic Worker Movement (Dorothy Day and Peter Maurin, United States, 1933)
		• Focolare Movement (Chiara Lubich, Italy, 1943)
		• Cursillo Movement (group of laymen, Spain, 1944)
		• *Comunione e Liberazione* (Fr. Luigi Guissani, Italy, 1954)
		• *Regnum Christi* (Fr. Marcial Maciel, LC, Mexico, 1959)
		• Neocatechumenal Way (*Redemptoris Mater*) (two laypeople, Spain, 1964)
		• Catholic Charismatic Renewal (two laymen, United States, 1967)
		• Sant'Egidio Community (group of high school students, Italy, 1968)
		• Families of Nazareth Movement (Fr. Tadeusz Dajczer, Poland, 1985)
		• Center for Contemplation and Action (Fr. Richard Rohr, OFM, United States, 1986)
		• ACTS Missions (three laymen, United States, 1986) – offshoot from the Cursillo Movement

The roots of the Church are very deep. For more than 2,000 years, prayer has nourished the life of the saints and all the disciples of Jesus. The above analysis demonstrates how the Eastern Christian spiritual tradition has essentially revolved around the Jesus Prayer, beginning with the Desert Fathers and Mothers, and continuing to modern times. Thus, this mystical tradition of the Christian East has been faithfully practiced and preserved since the time of the Early Church.

In contrast, a number of spiritual traditions emerged in the West. During the Scholastic Period, there was essentially a separation between theology and spirituality, as the study of theology migrated from monasteries to universities, where it became a rigorous academic discipline. The same separation did not occur in the Christian East, wherein knowledge of God was based on actual experience. The maxim of Evagrius Ponticus is often quoted by Orthodox Theologians: "If you are a theologian you truly pray. If you truly pray you are a theologian."[413]

A significant shift occurred at the Second Vatican Council, which espoused *ressourcement*—a return to the sources. This generally meant a shift away from Scholasticism with a renewed emphasis on Sacred Scripture and the Patristic sources. The writings of Karl Rahner, SJ, for example, reflect this shift: "The devout Christian of the future will either be a 'mystic,' one who has 'experienced' something, or he [she] will cease to be anything at all."[414]

The great beauty of the Universal Catholic Church is that it includes the spiritual patrimony of both East and West. Pope St. John Paul II believed the Church needed to learn to breathe again from both lungs, one Eastern and one Western.[415] Recent popes

---

413 Evagrius Ponticus, *The Praktikos & Chapters on Prayer*, 65. Also found in *The Philokalia*, vol. 1, 62.

414 Karl Rahner, "Christian Living Formerly and Today," in *Theological Investigations*, vol. VII (New York: Seabury Press, 1972), 15.

415 Pope St. John Paul II often spoke of the need for the Church to achieve its deepest meaning by breathing from both its lungs, one Eastern and one Western. See for example *Ut Unum Sint* (Rome: Libreria Editrice Vaticana, 1995), no. 54.

have described the need to rediscover the treasures of the Eastern Catholic Churches in order to create a true synthesis reflective of the Universal Catholic Church. On a similar note, Cardinal Sarah writes, "The spiritual and cultural heritage of the Russian Orthodox Church is unequaled. The reawakening of faith that followed the fall of Communism is an immense hope. It is the fruit of the blood of martyrs."[416] Further, "in Russia, the Orthodox Church has to a great extent resumed its pre-1917 role as the moral foundation of society."[417]

One could make similar observations about the Church in Ukraine, Slovakia, Hungary, and Romania, essentially arising from the catacombs, having remained alive and vibrant during Communist repression and preserving the Deposit of Faith, often at great price. These Eastern Christian experiences and perspectives provide a further richness to our Catholic faith, especially related to mysticism, the theology of encounter, and the hesychast prayer tradition (Jesus Prayer). Encounter is essential to establishing a deep-seated relationship with Jesus Christ, the source of life, hope, and way to eternal blessedness.

With this emphasis on encounter, we begin to appreciate the spirituality of such people as Mother Teresa of Calcutta, who asks us the right question, "Do you really know the living Jesus—not from books but from being with him in your heart?"[418] Her entire apostolate to the poor and suffering was anchored in contemplative prayer. Thus, one critical aspect of the spiritual journey, to know God's plan for us, we must come to know and love his Son, Jesus Christ. One way we come to know him is through prayer. Recall the teaching of Isaac the Syrian, "You cannot taste honey by reading a book." To know Jesus is to experience him.

---

416 Robert Cardinal Sarah, *The Day is Now Far Spent*, 239.
417 Ibid., 240.
418 Mother Teresa, "Jesus is My All," edited by Fr. Brian Kolodiejchuk, MC (San Diego, CA: Mother Teresa Center, 2005), 13.

For further information and a concise history of Christian spirituality including Protestant traditions, the following text is recommended:

Sheldrake, Philip. *Spirituality: A Concise History*. 2nd ed. West Sussex, UK: John Wiley-Blackwell, 2013.

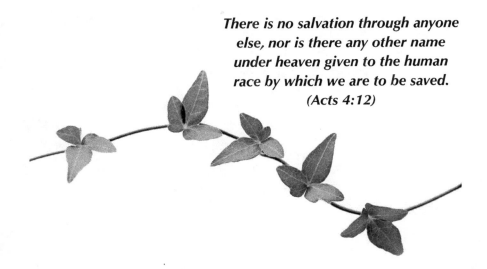

There is no salvation through anyone else, nor is there any other name under heaven given to the human race by which we are to be saved.
(Acts 4:12)

Bibliography

Aimilianos of Simonopetra, Archimandrite. *The Church at Prayer*. Edited by The Holy Convent of the Annunciation, Ormylia. Alhambra, CA: Sebastian Press, 2012.

Anderson, Elizabeth. "How Spiritual Direction Transformed a Catholic High School." *National Catholic Reporter* online (February 6, 2019).

Art of Prayer, The. Compiled by Igumen Chariton. Translated by E. Kadloubovsky and G. E. H. Palmer. London: Farrar, Straus and Giroux, 1966.

Ascetical Homilies of Saint Isaac the Syrian, The. Translated by Holy Transfiguration Monastery. 2nd rev. ed. Brookline, MA: Holy Transfiguration Monastery, 2011.

Balan, Archimandrite Ioanichie. *Elder Cleopa of Sihastria*. Translated by Mother Cassiana. Lake George, CO: New Varatec Publishing, 2001.

Bebis, George S. "Nikodimos of the Holy Mountain," *Encyclopedia of Religion* Edited by Lindsay Jones. 2nd ed., vol. 10. Detroit: Macmillan Reference USA, 2005, 6621. *Gale Virtual Reference Library*. Web. Sept. 27, 2014.

Benedict XVI, Pope. *Porta Fidei—Door of Faith: Apostolic Letter of the Supreme Pontiff for the Indiction of the Year of Faith*. Rome: Libreria Editrice Vaticana, 2012.

Brianchaninov, Ignatius. *The Field: Cultivating Salvation*. Translated by Nicholas Kotar. Jordanville, NY: Holy Trinity Publications, 2016.

———. *The Refuge: Anchoring the Soul in God*. Translated by Nicholas Kotar. Jordanville, NY: Holy Trinity Publications, 2019.

Breck, John. "Prayer of the Heart: Sacrament of the Presence of God," *St. Vladimir's Theological Quarterly* 29, no. 1 (1995): 25–45.

Bunge, Gabriel, OSB. *Earthen Vessels: The Practice of Personal Prayer According to the Patristic Tradition*. San Francisco, CA: Ignatius Press, 2002.

Callistus and Ignatius of Xanthopoulos. "Directions to Hesychasts." Taken from *Writings from the Philokalia on Prayer of the Heart*. Translated by E. Kadloubovsky and G.E.H. Palmer. London: Faber and Faber, 1992. 164-270.

Catechism of the Catholic Church. 2nd.Ed. Revised in accordance with the official Latin text promulgated by Pope John Paul II. Rome: Libreria Editrice Vaticana, 1997.

Catholic News Service. "Young Adults Want to be Heard by the Church, Study Finds." *Texas Catholic Herald*, January 23, 2018.

Chaput, Charles J., OFM Cap. *Living the Catholic Faith: Rediscovering the Basics*. Cincinnati, OH: St. Anthony Messenger Press, 2001.

———. *Strangers in a Strange Land: Practicing the Catholic Faith in a Post-Christian World*. New York: Henry Holt, 2017.

Chrysologus, St. Peter. "Sermon 43." Taken from *The Liturgy of the Hours*, vol. II. New York: Catholic Book Publishing Company, 1976. 231-232.

Chrysostom, St. John. *De Precatione*, Homily 6. Taken from *The Liturgy of the Hours*, vol. 2. New York: The Catholic Book Publishing Company, 1976. 68-70.

———. "Gospel of Matthew," Homily 50. Taken from *The Liturgy of the Hours*, vol. IV. New York: The Catholic Book Publishing Company, 1975. 182-183.

Chryssavgis, John. *In the Heart of the Desert: The Spirituality of the Desert Fathers and Mothers*. Bloomington, IN: World Wisdom, Inc., 2003.

Climacus, St. John. *The Ladder of Divine Ascent*. Translated by Colm Luibheid and Norman Russell. New York: Paulist Press, 1982.

Colossians, 1-2 Thessalonians, 1-2 Timothy, Titus, Philemon. Edited by Peter Gorday. From "Ancient Christian Commentary on Scripture" series, NT, vol. IX. Downers Grove, IL: InterVarsity Press, 2000.

Coniaris, Anthony M. *Achieving Your Potential in Christ: Theosis*. Minneapolis: Light & Life Publishing Company, 2004.

———. *Tools for Theosis: Becoming God-like in Christ*. Minneapolis, MN: Light & Life Publishing Company, 2014.

Deacon and Pilgrim. *Hearts Afire: Fulfilling Our Destiny*. 2nd ed. Fairfax, VA: Eastern Christian Publications, 2014.

DeBona, Guerric, OSB. *Preaching Effectively, Revitalizing Your Church*. New York/Mahwah, NJ: Paulist Press, 2009.

Divine Liturgies of Our Holy Fathers John Chrysostom and Basil the Great. The. Pittsburgh: Byzantine Seminary Press, 2006.

Dorotheos of Gaza. *Discourses and Sayings*. Translated by Eric P. Wheeler. Kalamazoo, MI: Cistercian Publications, 1977.

Elizabeth of the Trinity, St., OCD. *I Have Found God*. Complete Works, vol. 1, "Major Spiritual Writings." Translated by Sr. Aletheia Kane, OCD. Washington, DC: ICS Publications, 2014.

Evagrius Ponticus. *The Praktikos & Chapters on Prayer*. Translated by John Eudes Bamberger, OCSO. Kalamazoo, MI: Cistercian Publications, 1972.

Francis, Pope. *Evangelii Gaudium*. Rome: Libreria Editrice Vaticana, 2013.

———. *Misericordiae Vultus*. Rome: Libreria Editrice Vaticana, 2015.

Hesychius of Jerusalem. "Texts on Sobriety and Prayer." Taken from *Writings from the Philokalia on Prayer of the Heart*. Translated by E. Kadloubovsky and G.E.H. Palmer. London: Faber and Faber, 1992. 279-321.

Hierotheos of Nafpaktos, Metropolitan. *A Night in the Desert of the Holy Mountain: Discussion with a Hermit on the Jesus Prayer*. Translated by Effie Mavromichali. Levadia, Greece: Birth of the Theotokos Monastery, 2009.

Hopko, Thomas. "Ioann of Kronstadt," *Encyclopedia of Religion*. Edited by Lindsay Jones. 2nd ed., vol. 7. Detroit: Macmillan Reference USA, 2005, 4532. Gale Virtual Reference Library. Web. Nov. 26, 2014.

John of Karpathos, St. "For the Encouragement of the Monks in India Who had written to Him: One Hundred Texts." Taken from *The Philokalia: The Complete Text*, vol. I. Translated by G.E.H. Palmer, P. Sherrard, and K. Ware. London: Faber & Faber, 1979. 298-321.

John of Kronstadt, St. *My Life in Christ*, Part 1 and Part 2. Translated by E. E. Goulaeff. Revised and adapted by Nicholas Kotar. Jordanville, NY: Holy Trinity Monastery, 2015.

_____., *My Life in Christ*. Translated by E. E. Goulaeff. Jordanville, NY: Holy Trinity Monastery, 2000.

John Paul II, Pope St. *Orientale Lumen*. Rome: Libreria Editrice Vaticana, 1995.

———. *Ut Unum Sint*. Rome: Libreria Editrice Vaticana, 1995.

Johnson, Luke Timothy. *The Gospel of Luke*. In the "Sacra Pagina" series, vol. 3. Collegeville, MN: Liturgical Press, 1991.

Kaisch, Ken. *Finding God: A Handbook of Christian Meditation*. New York: Paulist Press, 1994.

Keating, Thomas, OCSO. *Intimacy with God*. New York: The Crossroad Publishing Company, 2002.

Keller, David G.R. *Desert Banquet: A Year of Wisdom from the Desert Fathers and Mothers*. Collegeville, MN: Liturgical Press, 2011.

Kelly, Matthew. *Rediscover the Saints*. Assam, India: Blue Sparrow Books, 2019.

Kleinguetl, Edward. *Encounter: Experiencing the Divine Presence*. Parker CO: Outskirts Press, 2018.

———. *Choosing Life in Christ: A Vocation to Holiness*. Parker, CO: Outskirts Press, 2019.

———. *Into the Desert: The Wisdom of the Desert Fathers and Mothers*. Parker, CO: Outskirts Press, 2019.

Lach, Most Rev. Milan, SJ. "A Year of Renewal." Pastoral Letter to the Faithful of the Byzantine Catholic Eparchy of Parma (January 6, 2019).

Laird, Martin, OSA. *Into the Silent Land: A Guide to the Christian Practice of Contemplation.* Oxford University Press, 2006.

Langford, Joseph, MC. *Mother Teresa's Secret Fire.* Huntington, IN: Our Sunday Visitor, 2008.

Maasburg, Leo. *Mother Teresa of Calcutta: A Personal Portrait.* Translated by Michael J. Miller. San Francisco: Ignatius Press, 2010.

Maloney, George A., SJ. *Prayer of the Heart: The Contemplative Tradition of the Christian East.* Notre Dame, IN: Ave Maria Press, 2008.

———. *St. Symeon the New Theologian: The Mystic of Fire & Light and Hymns of Divine Love.* IJA Publications, 2011.

Mark the Ascetic, St. "On Those Who Think That They are Made Righteous by Works: Two Hundred and Twenty-Six Texts." *The Philokalia: The Complete Text*, vol. 1. Compiled by St. Nikodimos of the Holy Mountain and St. Makarios of Corinth. Translated and edited by G.E.H. Palmer, Philip Sherrard, and Kallistos Ware. New York: Faber and Faber, 1983. 125-146.

Martini, Gabe. "Carrying the Cross and Suffering in Hope" *On Behalf of All* online. http://onbehalfofall.org/carrying-the-cross-and-suffering-in-hope.

McCarty, Robert J. and John M. Vitek. *Going, Going, Gone: The Dynamics of Disaffiliation in Young Catholics.* Winona, MN: St. Mary's Press, 2017.

"Monasticism: VI. Eastern Monasticism Since 1453," *New Catholic Encyclopedia Supplement 2010.* Edited by Robert L. Fastiggi, vol. 2. Detroit: Gale, 2010, 817-821. *Gale Virtual Reference Library.* Web. Sept. 24, 2014. 821.

Monk of Mount Athos, A. *The Watchful Mind: Teachings on the Prayer of the Heart.* Translated by George Dokos. Yonkers, NY: St. Vladimir's Seminary Press, 2014.

Moschonas, Anthony. Post by Alexander Poshtaruk. *Face Book*, "Ask About the Orthodox Faith." December 10, 2019.

Moses, Monk, of Mount Athos. *Athonite Flowers: Seven Contemporary Essays on the Spiritual Life*. Translated by Fr. Peter A. Chamberas. Brookline, MA: Holy Cross Press, 2000.

———. *Holiness: Is It Attainable Today?* Translated by Fr. Peter A. Chamberas. Brookline, MA: Holy Cross Orthodox Press, 2012.

Nolan, Albert. *Jesus Before Christianity*. Maryknoll, NY: Orbis Books, 2013.

Paisios of Mount Athos, Elder. *Passions and Virtues*. Taken from "Spiritual Counsels," vol. V. Translated by Peter Chamberas. Edited by Anna Famellos and Eleftheria Kaimakliotis. Souroti, Thessaloniki, Greece: Holy Monastery of Evangelist John the Theologian, 2016.

———. Paisios of Mount Athos, Elder. *Spiritual Struggles*. Taken from "Spiritual Counsels," vol. III. Translated by Peter Chamberas. Edited by Anna Famellos and Andrinikos Masters. Souroti, Thessaloniki, Greece: Holy Monastery of Evangelist John the Theologian, 2014.

Pilgrim's Tale, The. Translated by T. Allan Smith. "Introduction" by Aleksei Pentkovsky. Mahwah, NJ: Paulist Press, 1999.

Porphyrios, Elder. *Wound by Love: The Life and Wisdom of Elder Porphyrios*. Edited by Sisters of the Holy Convent of Chrysopigi. Translated by John Raffan. Limni, Evia, Greece: Denise Harvey, 2013.

"Prayer of St. Teresa of Ávila." www.ewtn.com/Devotionals/prayers/StTeresaofAvila.htm.

Rahner, Karl, SJ. "Christian Living Formerly and Today," *Theological Investigations*, vol. VII. New York: Seabury Press, 1972.

Rite of Penance. Totowa, NJ: Catholic Book Publishing Corp, 2009.

Sakharov, Archimandrite Sophrony. *St. Silouan the Athonite*. Translated by Rosemary Edmonds. Crestwood, NY: St. Vladimir's Seminary Press, 1991.

Sarah, Robert Cardinal, in conversation with Nicolas Diat. *The Day is Now Far Spent*. Translated by Michael J. Miller. San Francisco, CA: Ignatius Press, 2019.

———. *God or Nothing*. Translated by Michael J. Miller. San Francisco, CA: Ignatius Press, 2015.

———. *The Power of Silence: Against the Dictatorship of Noise*. Translated by Michael J. Miller. San Francisco: Ignatius Press, 2017.

Sayings of the Desert Fathers, The. Translated by Benedicta Ward, SLG. Kalamazoo, MI: Cistercian Publications, 1975.

Scalia, Elizabeth. "Exile: The Past is Prologue," *Patheos* online (April 3, 2009).

Schneiders, Sandra M. "Religion vs. Spirituality: A Contemporary Conundrum," *Spiritus: A Journal of Christian Spirituality* 3, no. 2 (2003): 169.

Second Vatican Council. *Lumen Gentium* (*Dogmatic Constitution of the Church*), solemnly promulgated by His Holiness Pope Paul VI on November 21, 1964. Boston: St. Paul Editions, 1965.

Sheldrake, Philip. *Spirituality: A Concise History*. 2nd ed. West Sussex, UK: John Wiley-Blackwell, 2013.

Stăniloae, Dumitru. *Revelation and Knowledge of the Triune God*. "The Experience of God" series, vol. 1. Translated and edited by Ioan Ionita and Robert Barringer. Brookline, MA: Holy Cross Orthodox Press.1998.

Symeon the New Theologian, St. *The Discourses* Translated by C.J. de Catanzaro. New York: The Paulist Press, 1980. 167-169.

———. "Holy Fasting," *Magnificat* 21, no. 12 (February 2020): 405-406.

Teresa, Mother. *Come Be My Light: The Private Writings of the 'Saint of Calcutta*. Edited and with commentary by Brian Kolodiejchuk, MC. New York: Doubleday, 2007.

———. "Jesus is My All." Edited by Fr. Brian Kolodiejchuk, MC. San Diego, CA: Mother Teresa Center, 2005.

———. *A Simple Path*. Compiled by Lucinda Vardey. (New York: Ballantine Books, 1995.

————. *Where There is Love, There is God*. Edited by Brian Kolodiejchuk, MC, and PhD. New York: Image Books, 2010.

Theophan the Recluse, St. *The Path to Salvation: A Concise Outline of Christian Ascesis*. Translated by Seraphim Rose. Stafford, AZ: Monastery of St. Paisius, 2016.

Unseen Warfare. Being the "Spiritual Combat" and "Path to Paradise" of Lorenzo Scupoli. Edited by Nicodemus of the Holy Mountain. Revised by Theophan the Recluse. Translated by E. Kadloubovsky and G. E. H. Palmer. Crestwood, NY: St. Vladimir's Seminary Press, 1963.

Ware, Metropolitan Kallistos Ware, "A Lecture on the Jesus Prayer." Presented on June 22, 2012, St. John the Baptist Cathedral (ROCOR). Washington, DC. http://myocn.net/metropolitan-kallistos-ware-jesus-prayer/.

Way of a Pilgrim and the Pilgrim Continues His Way. Translated by Helen Bacovcin. New York: Image Books Doubleday, 1978.

Wikipedia, The Free Encyclopedia, s.v. "Catholic Spirituality."

Wright, Paul A., MD. *Mother Teresa's Prescription: Finding Happiness and Peace in Service*. Notre Dame, IN: Ave Maria Press, 2006.

Zander, Valentine, *St. Seraphim of Sarov*. Translated by Sr. Gabriel Anne, SSC. Crestwood, NY: St. Vladimir's Seminary Press, 1975.

Acknowledgments

Revising this work on the Jesus Prayer was inspired by a number of people and sources. First, we would like to acknowledge His Excellency Bishop Joseph E. Strickland of the Diocese of Tyler, a courageous voice in our Church today, who zealously upholds the Deposit of Faith and who believes in the importance of a renewed focus on prayer. The image of you on your knees during the entire rosary, leading a

group in prayer for the renewal of the Church outside the hotel during the USCCB Meeting in Baltimore in cold and blustery conditions, is a great witness to all as to the importance of prayer.[419] You have been a refreshing voice who speaks to his brother bishops about staying true to orthodox teachings of the faith and the urgency to more readily proclaim the Good News of the Gospel. Thank you for your courage and conviction, so needed in the Church by its shepherds today. This book is dedicated to you in grateful appreciation and thanksgiving.

---

419 See Doug Mainwaring, "After US bishops Debate Downplaying Abortion, Bp. Strickland Leads Rosary Outside," *LifeSiteNews* online, November 14, 2019.

Second, we would like to acknowledge His Grace Bishop Milan Lach, SJ of the Eparchy of Parma (Ruthenian Byzantine Catholic), who has been calling his faithful to spiritual renewal and says his primary role as bishop is to teach his people how to pray. He is committed to a revival of interest in the Church Fathers, helping others to discover or be renewed in the Art of Spiritual Life, including ascetical practices and praying in the tradition of the Eastern Church Fathers (the Jesus Prayer). We pray that he will be the spark to set the earth on fire (Luke 12:49), because the American Church desperately needs the spiritual treasures of the Eastern Catholic Churches, particularly its mystical spiritual tradition of encounter and *theosis*. Hopefully, this book will be one more tool for assisting the faithful in learning how to pray in the Patristic tradition.

Third, we would like to acknowledge the inspiration provided by Metropolitan Archbishop Fülöp Kocsis of Hajdúdorog (Hungary). His Eminence attended the golden anniversary celebration for the establishment of the Eparchy of Parma in June 2019 and, when asked by a seminarian for his advice regarding formation of men preparing for priestly ministry, he referenced the wisdom of the Desert Fathers: "Go to your cell. Pray in your room. You know the Jesus Prayer? It is important to learn the Prayer of the Heart." Within the Hungarian Greek Catholic Church, there are three eparchies: the Archeparchy of Hajdúdorog and two suffragan eparchies. All of these are under the direction of bishops who are monks formed in the East Christian tradition, indicative of the bishops and spiritual fathers of the Early Church. As shepherds, their primary focus has been on the spiritual renewal of their people, which has created a fervor of faith and growth that is a model worthy of our consideration.

This book is part of a series of books, all of which have been themed around the Eastern Christian doctrine of *theosis*. This is the incremental process of transformation, becoming more Christ-like, preparing ourselves for our ultimate destiny—eternal blessedness (union with God). The initial inspiration for this corpus was His

Grace Bishop John M. Kudrick, Bishop Emeritus of the Eparchy of Parma. He had a great desire for his flock to be well-grounded in the beauty of their heritage and, when he expressed a desire to have an "Americanized" version of the *Theosis* Retreats, this entire effort was set into motion. Your Grace, with your assignment to the Monastery of Christ the Bridegroom, we hope you will be able to create a spiritual oasis and school of prayer. The Church desperately needs true spiritual fathers like you, holy men who can lead us closer to Christ.

Three Hierachs (L-R):
- *Bishop Milan Lach, SJ, Eparchy of Parma*
- *Bishop John Kudrick, Eparchy of Parma, Bishop Emeritus*
- *Metropolitan Fülöp Kocsis of Hajdúdorog*

We would like to thank His Eminence Robert Cardinal Sarah for his courage. As he wrote in his latest work, "This book is the cry of my soul!"[420] With this regard, he said:

> It wounds me to see so many pastors selling off Catholic doctrine and sowing seeds of division among

---

420 Cardinal Robert Sarah, *The Day is Now Far Spent*, 15.

> the faithful. We owe the Christian people clear, firm, stable teaching. How can we accept bishops' conferences that contradict each other? Where confusion reigns, God cannot dwell![421]

Thank you for speaking out and also reminding us of the prioritization of personal sanctification. Your books *God or Nothing*, *The Power of Silence*, and *The Day is Now Far Spent* have influenced this work. We hope many will be inspired by your heartfelt words of wisdom and concern for the Church.

We would like to thank His Grace Archbishop Charles J. Chaput, OFM Cap of Philadelphia, whose books *Living the Catholic Faith* and *Strangers in a Strange Land* have been a great source of inspiration. His Grace remains a constant voice against complacency in the American Church, has consistently stood in opposition to the dilution of faith and Church teachings, and is continuously recognized as one of the most trusted and admired bishops of our time.

I would like to acknowledge and thank Fr. Miron Kerul-Kmec for his continuous support, encouragement, and spiritual counsel. He has accompanied me on my spiritual journey and has been a great inspiration. He also has a great desire to lead his community closer to Christ, guiding them in terms of a renewal of the interior life (the Art of Spiritual Life, as he has named it), reflecting on the teachings of the Eastern Fathers of the Church. He is a true shepherd and spiritual father who epitomizes my favorite model of Church, *sobornost*—the church at the center of the village, drawing all people together, a beacon of light and hope. Just as God should be at the center of our lives, so should the parish church be at the heart of our communities. Fr. Miron's passion for evangelization bears witness to his understanding of the true mission of a parish community: to help its members come to know and love Jesus Christ, to accompany them on the spiritual journey, and to prepare them

---

421 Ibid., 17.

for eternal blessedness; the life that is to come. While the challenges of evangelization in light of the dominant culture are great and support often seems lacking, I pray that you never lose your zeal for the salvation of souls. You are a great spiritual father, truly an embodiment of the Patristic Fathers of the Early Church. I am so grateful to Fr. Miron, his wife Marcelka, and the members of St. Nicholas Byzantine Catholic Church in Barberton, Ohio, for being such a welcoming community. They are proof of what a vibrant parish can truly be like.

Fr. Deacon Miron Kerul-Kmec, Jr. will be an excellent priest. He understands the importance of the interior life. The Church needs true spiritual fathers and, as was his own father, Miron will be one, too, I am certain. The journey has not been without its share of crosses. However, suffering perfects our faith and prepares us for the road ahead. May Christ continue to form you after his own heart, may the Holy Spirit direct your steps, and may the wisdom of the Church Fathers provide the example of perseverance in imitation of Christ. Also, I want to acknowledge his wife and future *presbytera*, Sarah Marie, and wish both of you much success and many blessings in your joint vocation. Thank you for your friendship and making me feel like part of your family.

I am also grateful to Donna Rueby, who envisioned the importance of planting and nurturing the seed of faith in our high school youth. She knew years ago the importance of silence and contemplation. Also, I want to thank Fr. Arthur Carrillo, CP, and Fr. Freddy Ocampo, CP, who have provided practical suggestions to this work. Thank you to Fr. Mark Goring, CC, for his passion for evangelization, especially through his YouTube videos, and in particular those that touch upon the Jesus Prayer. He is outspoken about the truth of the Gospel, encouraging others to deepen their spiritual life, to pursue virtue, and to shun compromise with the spirit of the age. *¡Viva Cristo Rey!*

Thank you to Julio Lago for his thoughtful insights and comments on this work. May God continue to guide you as you discern a vocation to the diaconate.

Others also encouraged me on my spiritual journey: My priest-mentor, Fr. Edward Zavell, adopted me as a young man in high school seminary and inflamed my passion for Byzantine Catholicism. And, where would one be in the Eastern Christian spiritual tradition without an outstanding Spiritual Father? For me, that person is Fr. Damon Geiger, who was my spiritual guide during my first three years of ordained ministry. He helped me delve much more deeply into the beauty of the Eastern Christian mystical tradition and first introduced me to the concept of *theosis*. What Fr. Ed planted, Fr. Damon cultivated by opening my eyes to the true beauty that lay beneath the ornate liturgies and traditions.

Sometimes we do not realize how much one individual has influenced us until much later. I am incredibly grateful to Fr. Nicholas Weibl who, when we met, was the rector of Holy Spirit Seminary in Toledo, Ohio. In his class during my third year, 1976-1977, he introduced me to the Jesus Prayer, Mount Athos, and the concept of the *staretz*. It was also the first time I heard of Mother Teresa of Calcutta and Dorothy Day of New York. These people, places, and concepts have significantly influenced my life over the years and have emerged in many of our works. Fr. Weibl set a foundation that I never fully appreciated at the time. Today, I am in awe as to what I had learned and say with heartfelt gratitude, "thank you."

Our youth are the future of our Church, the ones to whom we are entrusted to pass along our spiritual treasures. They truly desire to know how to pray and to understand the Catholic faith they profess.

Speaking of prayer, I am grateful to the seven sisters of the Carmel Monastery of the Holy Trinity in New Caney, Texas, who regularly pray for me. In particular, I am grateful to Sr. Josefina of the Trinity, OCD, and Sr. Mary Theresa of the Eucharist, OCD, who encourage me to write. Thank you for your witness and prayers.

Finally, there were many others along the journey who provided input, inspiration, proofreading, and other helpful suggestions and support. I would specifically like to thank Gene Kirsch for his passion and enthusiasm in presenting his own witness about developing a personal relationship with Jesus and perspectives on prayer. His inputs to this effort have been invaluable.

To all the servants of God who influenced this work—His Eminence Cardinal Sarah, His Eminence Metropolitan Archbishop Fülöp, His Grace Archbishop Charles, His Grace Bishop Milan, His Grace Bishop John, His Excellency Bishop Joseph, Fr. Miron, Pani Marcelka, Fr. Deacon Miron, Jr., his wife and future *presbytera* Sarah Marie, the parishioners of St. Nicholas Byzantine Catholic Church in Barberton, Ohio, Fr. Arthur, Fr. Freddy, Fr. Mark, Fr. Damon, Fr. Nicholas, Sr. Josefina, Sr. Mary Theresa, Donna, Julio, Gene and his daughters Kathrine, Nicole, and Kimberly, the youth of our parishes, and all others, too numerous to mention — may God grant you many blessed years in peace, health, and happiness. *Mnohaja I blahaja lita.*

To my priest-mentor, Fr. Ed, may God grant him eternal memory and blessed repose. *Vičnaja jemu pamjat'.*

Christ is risen!

Fr. Deacon Edward Kleinguetl
Fr. Deacon Edward Kleinguetl, MASp
April 12, 2020
Feast of the Resurrection of Our Lord, God, and Savior Jesus Christ

> **We desire silence to hear in crystal**
> **purity the voice of Christ.**[422]
>
> —Elder Porphyrios of Kavsokalyvia

Recommended Further Reading and Reference

There are many rich texts from the Tradition, from the Church Fathers and Mothers. Below, we have included a few suggested works as a starting point for those who are interested, all of which we consider "reader friendly." We have included other sources of information as well.

Books

Aleksiev, Seraphim. *The Forgotten Medicine: The Mystery of Repentance.* Translated by Ralitsa Doynova. Wildwood, CA: St. Xenia Skete Press. 1994.

The Art of Prayer: An Orthodox Anthology. Compiled by Igumen Chariton of Valamo. Edited by Timothy Ware. Translated by E. Kadloubovsky and E.M. Palmer. London: Faber & Faber. 1997.[423]

Brianchaninov, Ignatius. *On the Prayer of Jesus.* Translated by Fr. Lazarus Moore. Boston: New Seeds Books. 2006.[424]

Hierotheos of Nafpaktos, Metropolitan. *A Night in the Desert of the Holy Mountain: Discussion with a Hermit on the Jesus Prayer.* Translated by Effie Mavromichali. Levadia, Greece: Birth of the Theotokos Monastery, 2009.

---

423 A significant number of the perspectives contained herein are by St. Theophan the Recluse.

424 Ignatius Brianchaninov (1807-1867) is a Russian monk and bishop. He provides a practical guide to the practice of the Jesus Prayer, drawing upon the writings of many spiritual fathers mentioned herein including St. John Climacus, St. Symeon the New Theologian, St. Gregory of Sinai, St. Nicephorus of Mount Athos, St. Nil Sorsky, and St. Seraphim of Sarov, to mention a few, along with frequent references to the Gospels and the *Philokalia.*

The Pilgrim's Tale. Translated by. T. Allan Smith, with an "Introduction" by Aleksei Pentkovsky. Mahwah, NJ: Paulist Press. 1999.[425]

Porphyrios, Elder. *Wound by Love: The Life and Wisdom of Elder Porphyrios*. Edited by Sisters of the Holy Convent of Chrysopigi. Translated by John Raffan. Limni, Evia, Greece: Denise Harvey. 2013.

Sakharov, Archimandrite Sophrony. *We Shall See Him As He Is*. Platina, CA; St. Herman of Alaska Brotherhood, 2006.

Book of Prayers

Publicans Prayer Book. 3rd ed. Boston: Sofia Press, 2017.

Movie

Mysteries of the Jesus Prayer. Norris Chumley and Rev. Dr. John A. McGuckin, 2011.

Podcasts

https://artofspirituallife.podbean.com/.

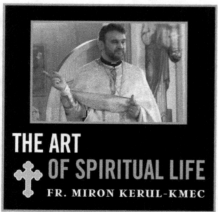

THE ART OF SPIRITUAL LIFE
FR. MIRON KERUL-KMEC

---

425 *The Pilgrim's Way:* There are other English translations, some known as *The Way of a Pilgrim*. The Paulist Press edition is translated from the oldest redaction of the work and a critical evaluation in the "Introduction" is provided by a professor from the Moscow Theological Academy of the Russian Orthodox Church.

Other Resources Available

(Listed in chronological order based on first edition)

Un Diácono y Peregrino. *Corazones en Llamas: Un Encuentro Personal con Jesús*. 2nd ed. Fairfax, VA: Eastern Christian Publications, 2016.

> Spanish. Discusses the ancient practice of the Jesus Prayer. Available at www.ecpubs.com. Imprimatur: His Eminence Daniel Cardinal DiNardo, Archbishop of Galveston-Houston.

A Deacon and Fellow Pilgrim. *Hearts Afire: Fulfilling Our Destiny*. 2nd ed. Fairfax, VA: Eastern Christian Publications, 2016.

> Discusses regaining the likeness of God (*theosis*) by reviewing selected passages of Sacred Scripture through a series of conferences and discussion questions. Available at www.ecpubs.com. Imprimatur: His Grace Bishop John Kudrick, Bishop Emeritus of the Eparchy of Parma (Ruthenian Byzantine Catholic).

Edward Kleinguetl. *Fulfilling Our Destiny: Theosis, Pope Francis, and the Jubilee of Mercy*. Jan. 2016.

> Parish Mission delivered at St. Nicholas Byzantine Catholic Church, Barberton, Ohio. Explores the Eastern Christian Doctrine of Theosis through the lens of Pope Francis's writings, especially *Evangelii Gaudium* and *Misericordiae Vultus*.
>
> Available online only at http://www.stnickbyz.com/pub/doc/archive/fod_retreat.pdf.

Edward Kleinguetl. *Encounter: Experiencing the Risen Jesus, Fulfilling Our Deepest Longing*. North Charleston, SC: CreateSpace, 2017.

> A theological framework considering the relevance of faith through a "spirituality of encounter." Available both in paperback or Kindle at www.amazon.com. Imprimatur: His Eminence Daniel Cardinal DiNardo, Archbishop of Galveston-Houston.

Edward Kleinguetl. *Encounter: Experiencing the Risen Jesus (A Retreat)*. North Charleston, SC: CreateSpace, 2017.

> A four-conference retreat addressing our ability to encounter the divine presence. Available at www.amazon.com.

Edward Kleinguetl. *Journey: Striving for Our Destiny*. North Charleston, SC: CreateSpace, 2017.

> Series of reflections on the ups and downs of the spiritual journey using the context of Holy Week. Available in paperback at www.amazon.com. Imprimatur: His Eminence Daniel Cardinal DiNardo, Archbishop of Galveston-Houston.

Edward Kleinguetl. *Encounter: Experiencing the Divine Presence*. Parker, CO: Outskirts Press, 2018.

> A series of conversations examining critical aspects of our faith by focusing on our experiences of encounters with the divine presence. Enriched by the Church's Eastern Christian patrimony, which retains a mystical tradition centered on the interior life and contemplative prayer. Imprimatur: His Eminence Daniel Cardinal DiNardo, Archbishop of Galveston-Houston.

Edward Kleinguetl. *Into the Desert: The Wisdom of the Desert Fathers and Mothers*. Parker, CO: Outskirts Press, 2019.

> A series of conferences structured as a retreat focusing on tried and true lessons from the Early Desert Dwellers, who modeled a very back-to-basics spirituality focused on cultivating a relationship with God. The lessons of the desert are equally relevant to today as they were in the ancient times of the Church. Available both in paperback and Kindle at www.amazon.com. Imprimatur: His Eminence Daniel Cardinal DiNardo, Archbishop of Galveston-Houston.

Edward Kleinguetl. *Choosing Life in Christ: A Vocation to Holiness*. Parker, CO: Outskirts Press, 2019.

> A series of conferences structured as a retreat focusing on responding to the call of Jesus, allowing him to form us on the journey to holiness. Includes a post-retreat conference on Evangelization. Available both in paperback and Kindle at www.amazon.com. Imprimatur: His Eminence Daniel Cardinal DiNardo, Archbishop of Galveston-Houston.

CPSIA information can be obtained
at www.ICGtesting.com
Printed in the USA
FSHW021643200720

9 781977 222879